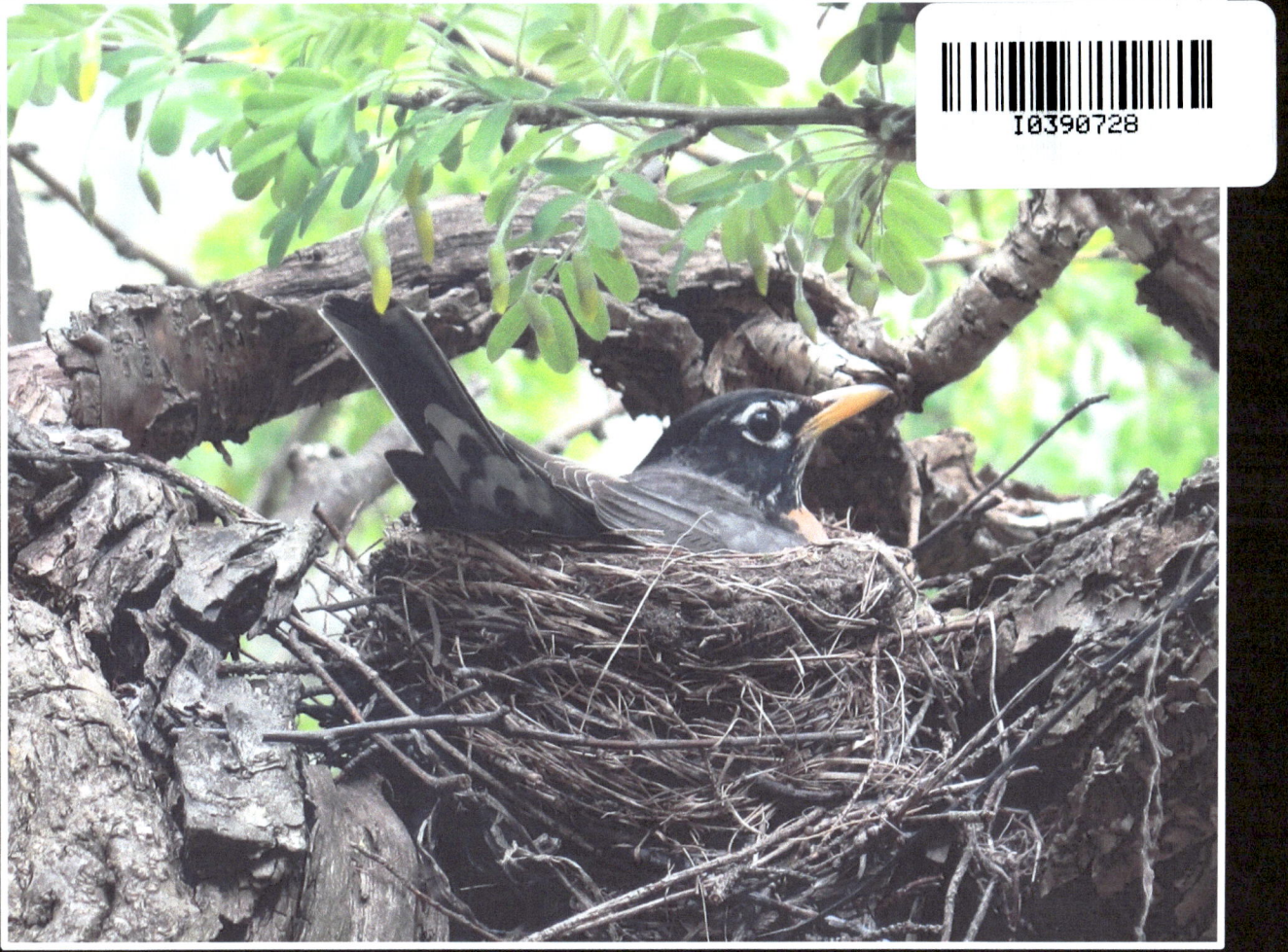

On a low branch of a small tree, a mother robin bird built a nest and laid four little blue eggs. After two weeks of sitting on those eggs, they were ready to hatch. I was very lucky to get my first peek inside the nest immediately after the first two chicks hatched. This is their story.

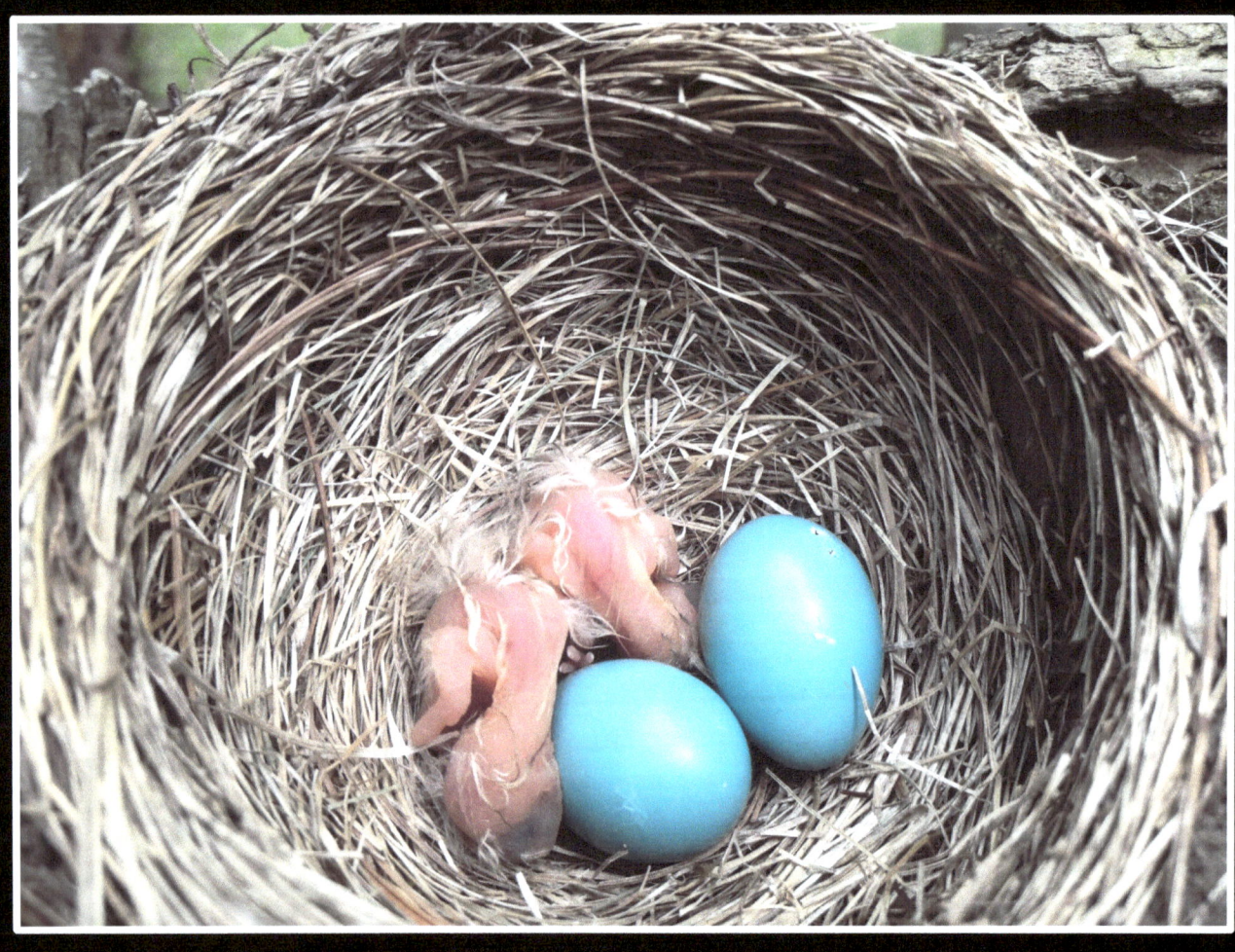

The first time I looked inside the nest was early in the morning, and this is what I saw. The chicks were brand new and their mother had already flown their eggshells away from the nest to distract predators (like squirrels, raccoons, snakes, or larger birds).

By early afternoon, the third chick was hatching too. It was pecking at the inside of its egg with a special little hook on its beak called an egg-tooth.

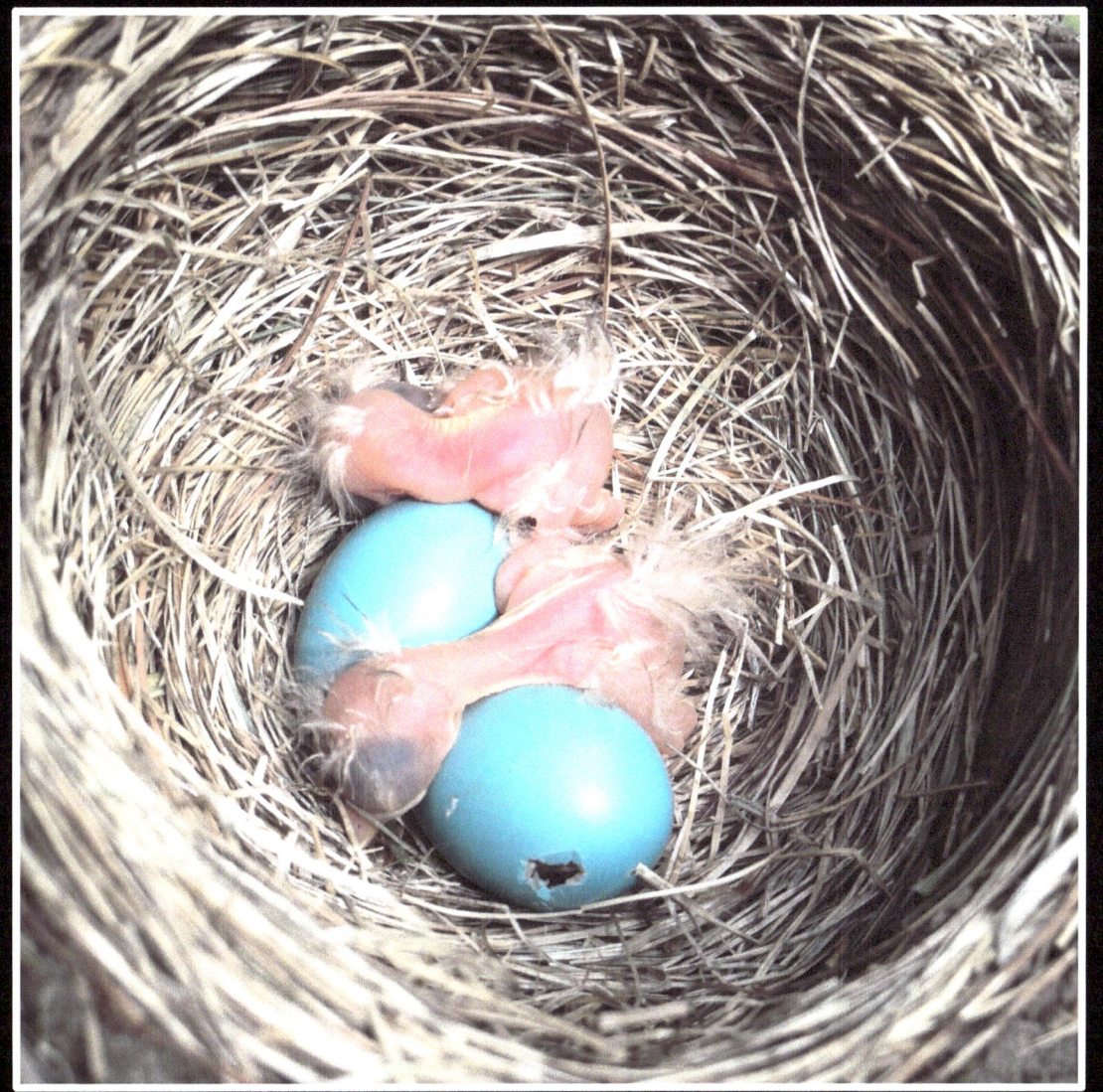

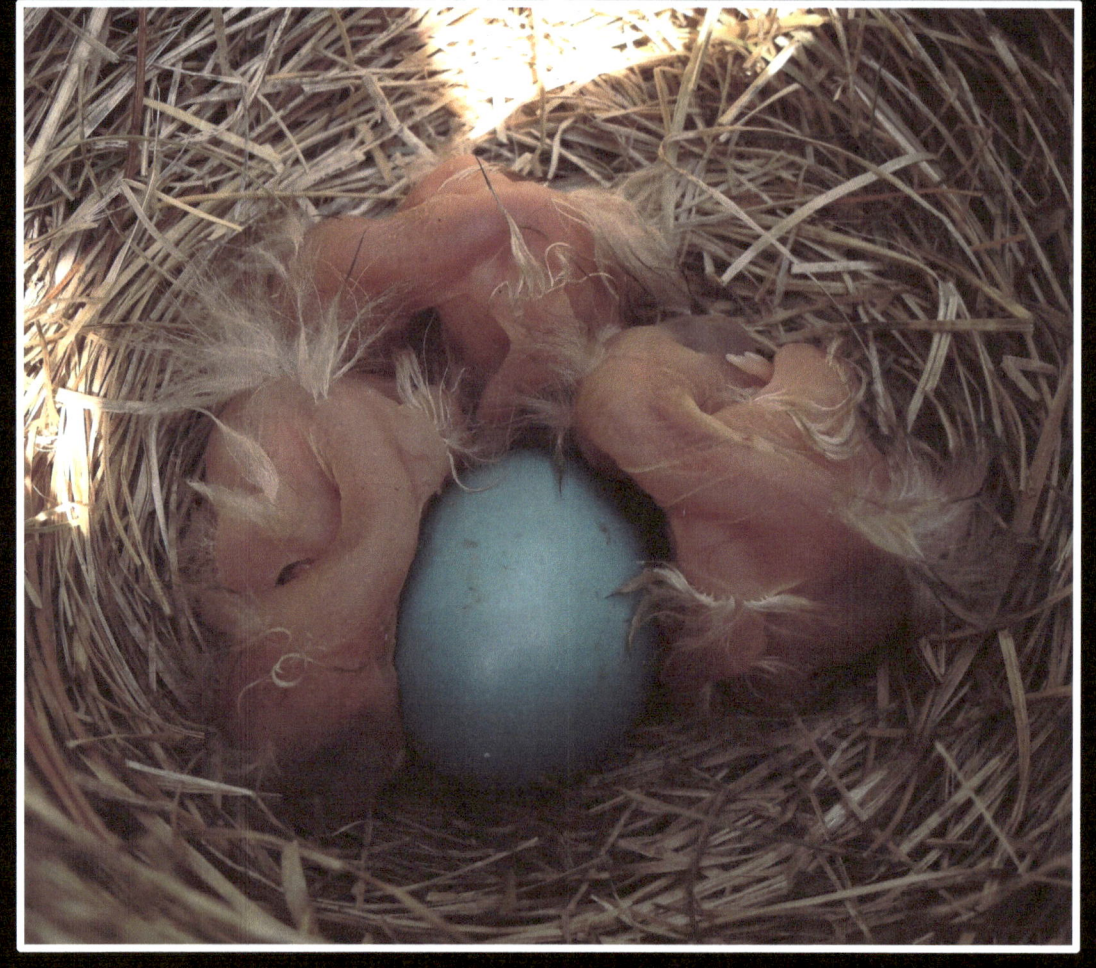

And then there were three!

That night there was a big rainstorm, but the mother robin sat tight on her nest with her wings spread out over all of her babies. She kept turning her last egg to keep the chick from sticking to the inside of its shell.

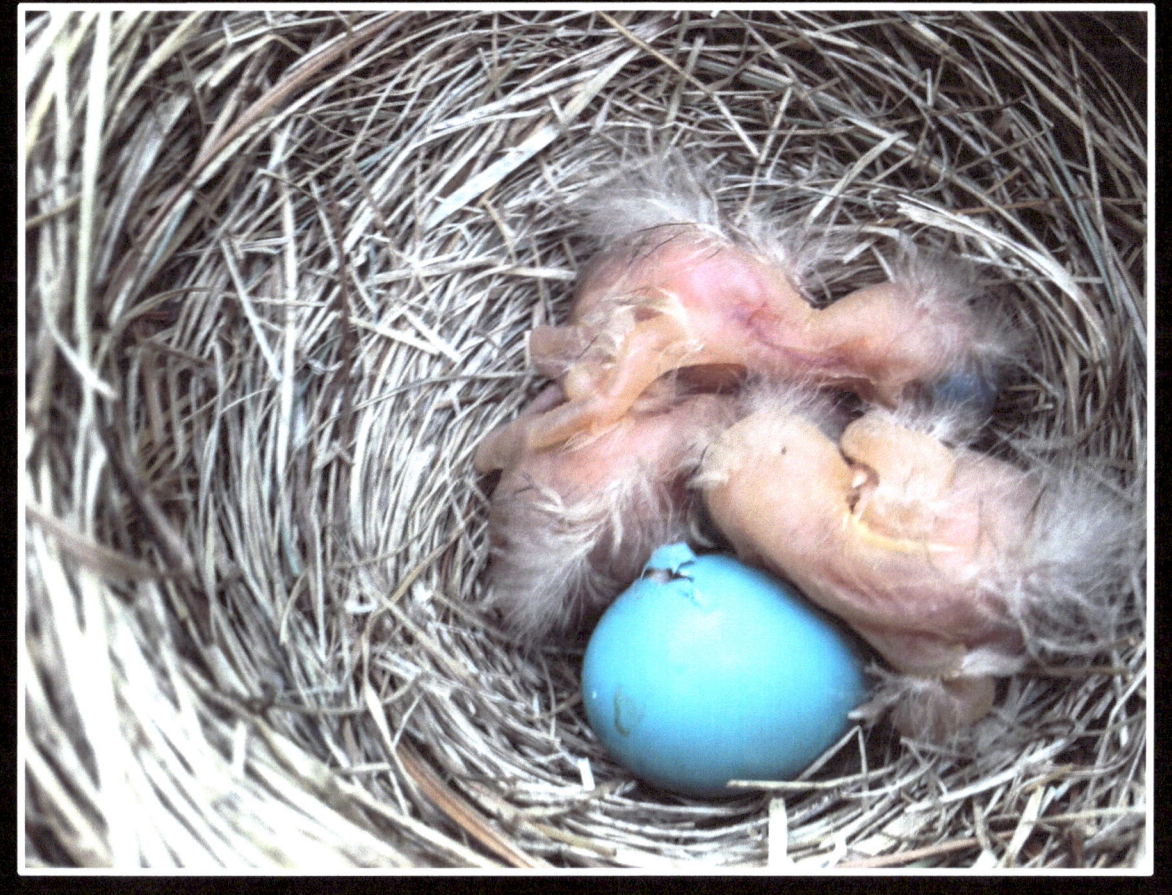

It took until the next morning for the fourth chick to hatch. Robins almost always lay four eggs and the eggs normally hatch in the order they were laid.

Two hours later there were four little chicks. Newly hatched robins look smaller and less developed than other birds because they spend less time growing inside the egg before they hatch.

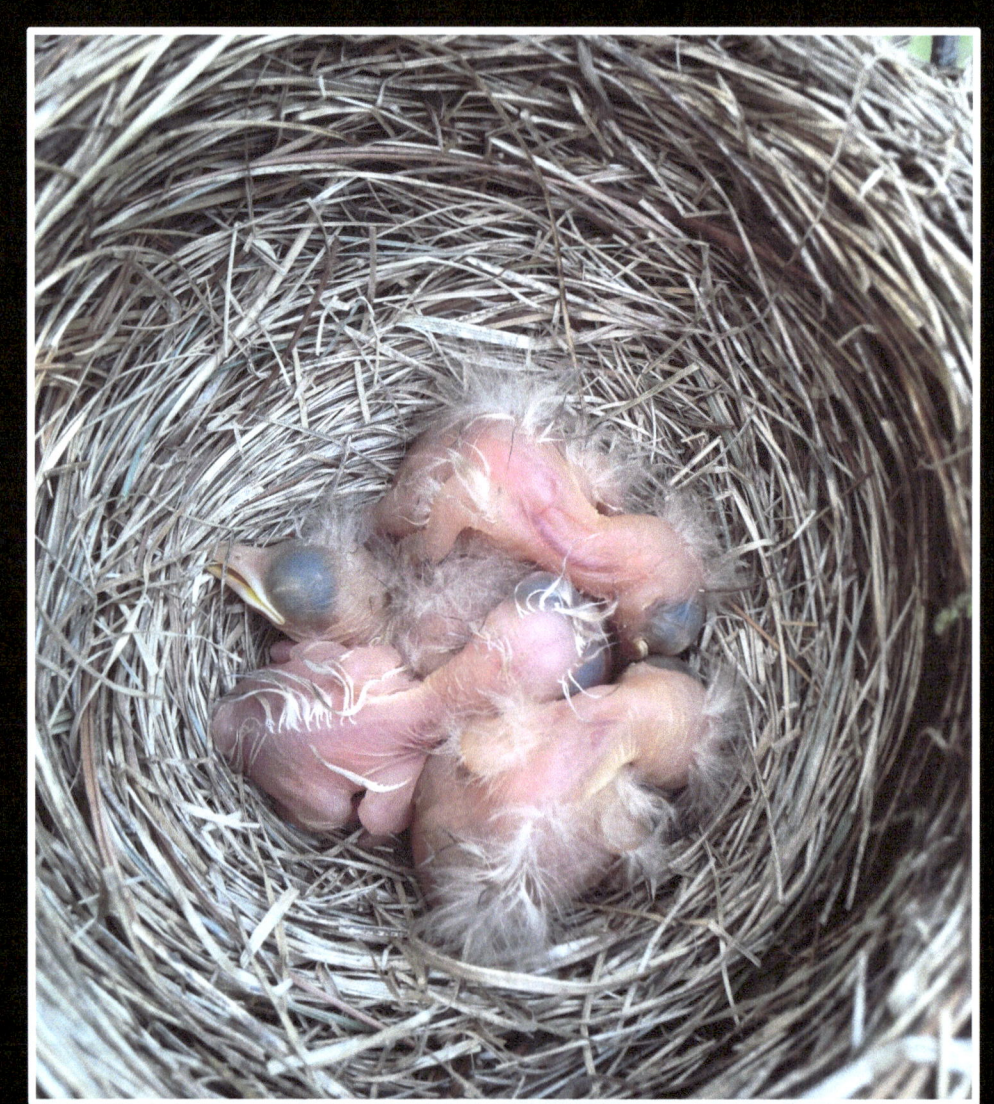

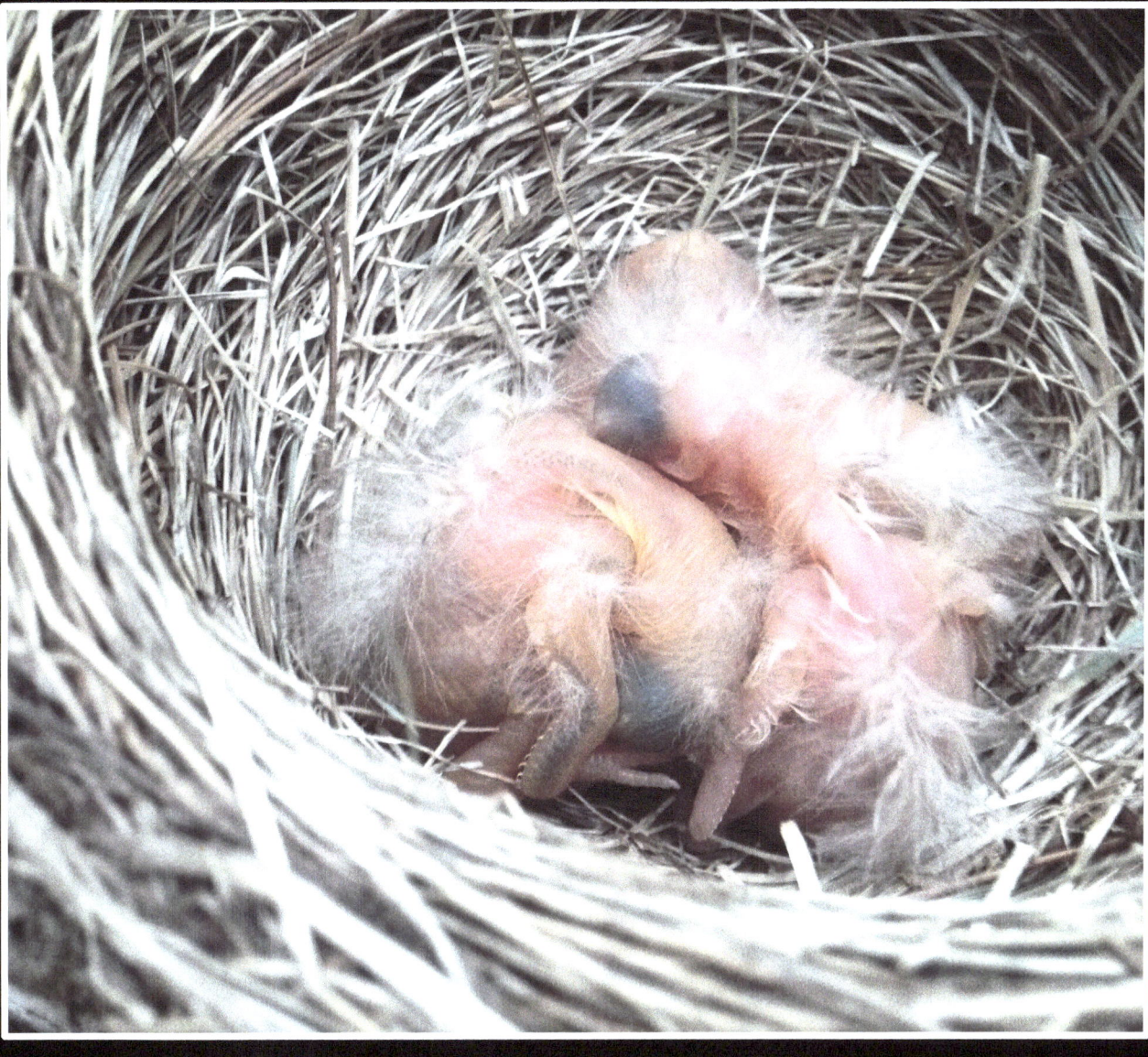

By night-time, all four chicks were snuggled up and keeping warm together. When chicks are too small to fly they are called nestlings. Nestlings need their mother to sit on them most of the day and night to keep them warm.

Both the mother and father robin birds watch over their nest. The parents of these chicks took turns finding food for their little nestlings and feeding them, and both swooped in and chirped loudly if anything got too close to their babies.

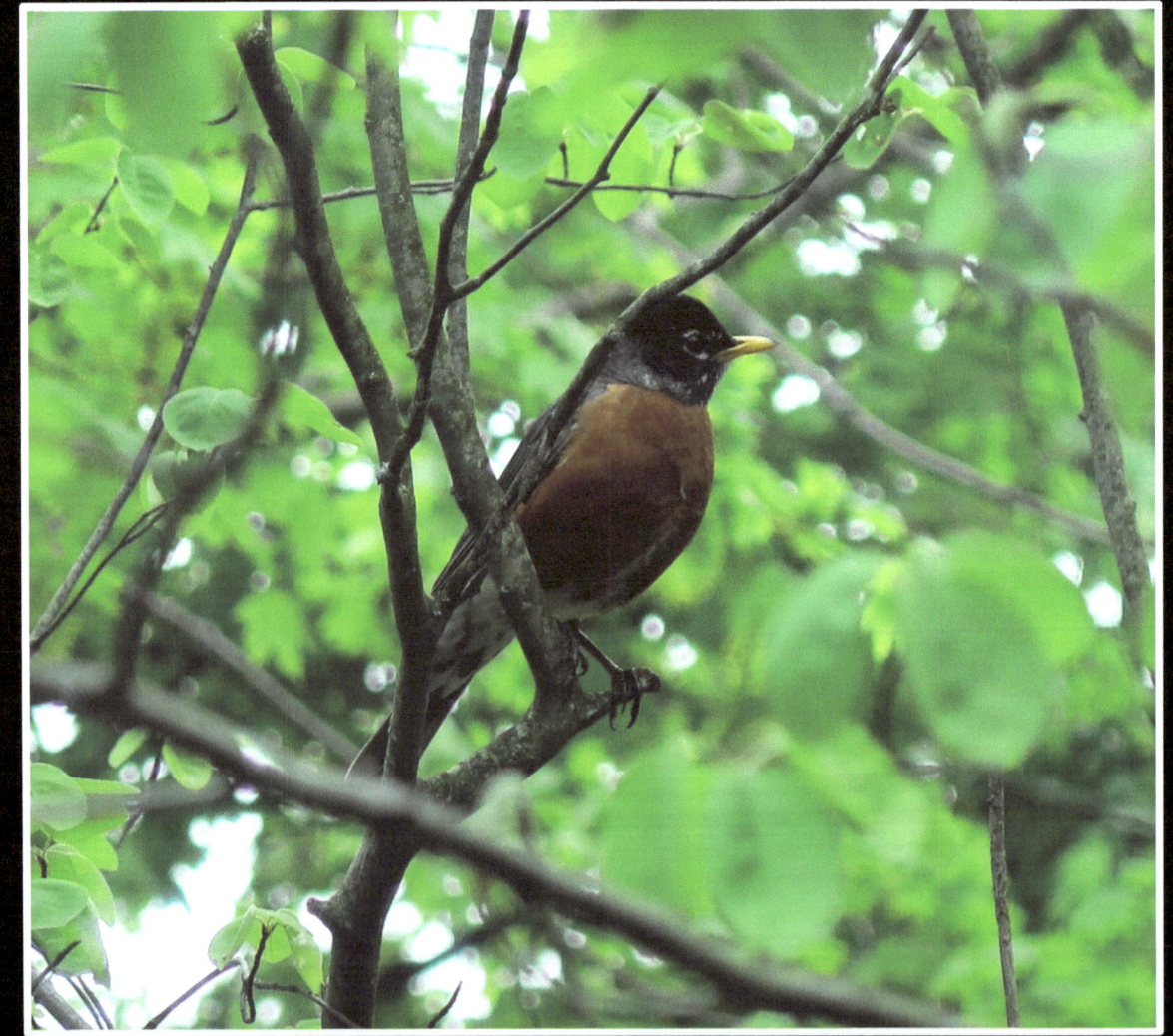

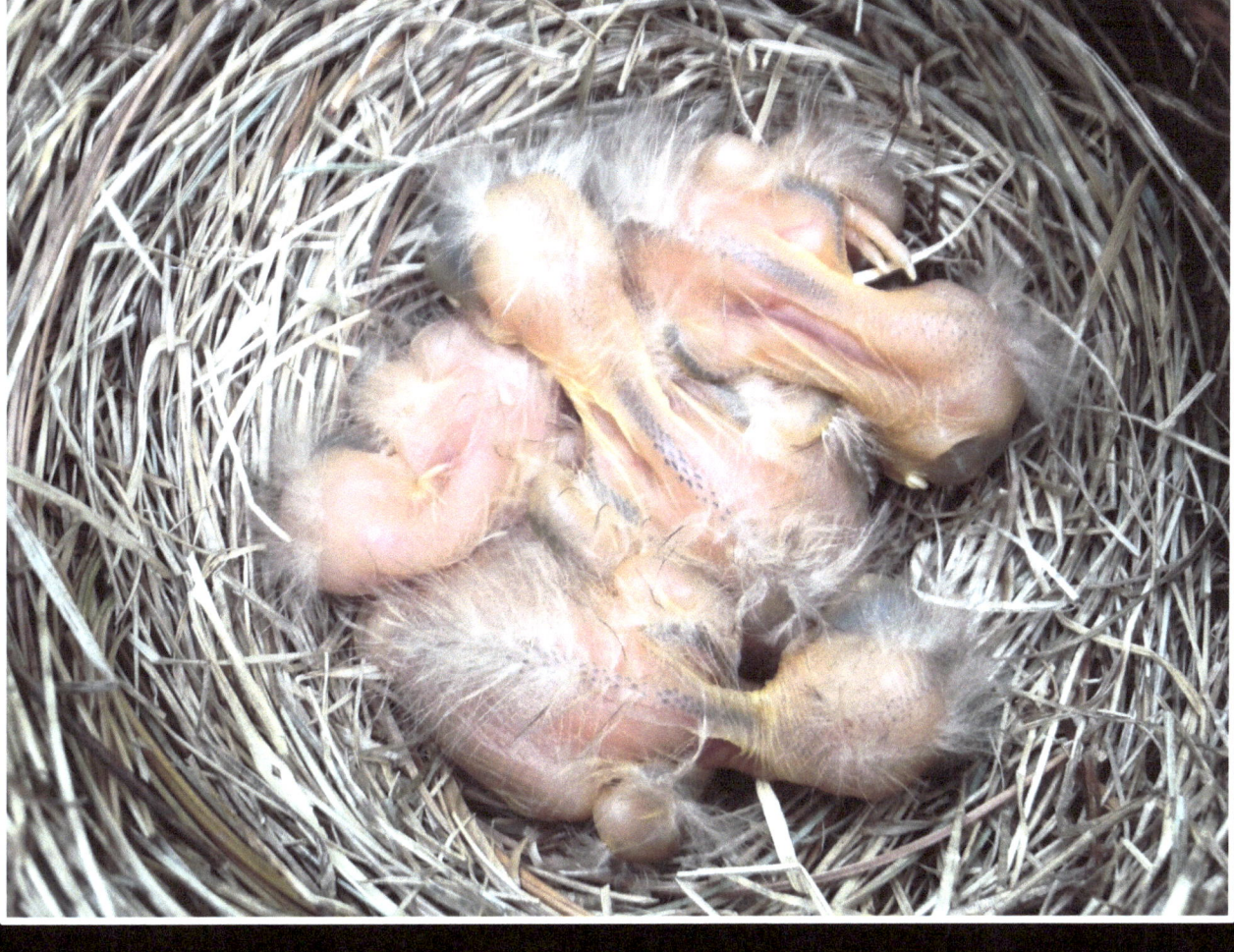

Despite the mother raccoon and her babies in the nearby tree, all four chicks were thriving by the start of the third morning.

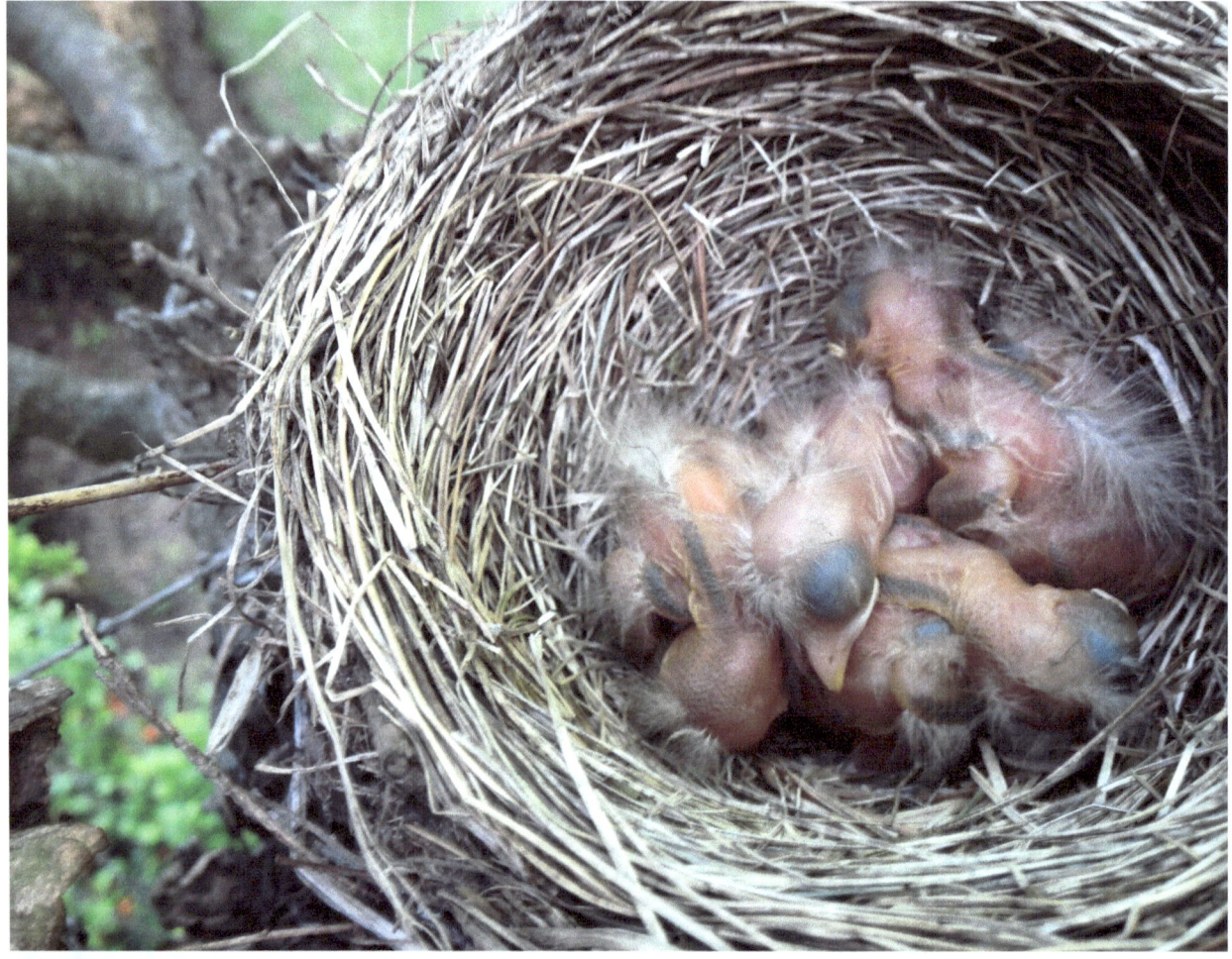

By the end of their third day, it was amazing to see how much the chicks had already changed. I had to be very careful not to scare away the parents or bother the babies.

There is a myth that robins can smell whether their chicks have been touched. Another myth about robins is that they hunt by smell or by tilting their heads to listen for worms. In truth, they tilt their heads to get a better view of the ground since they use their good eyesight to hunt for their prey.

DAY 4

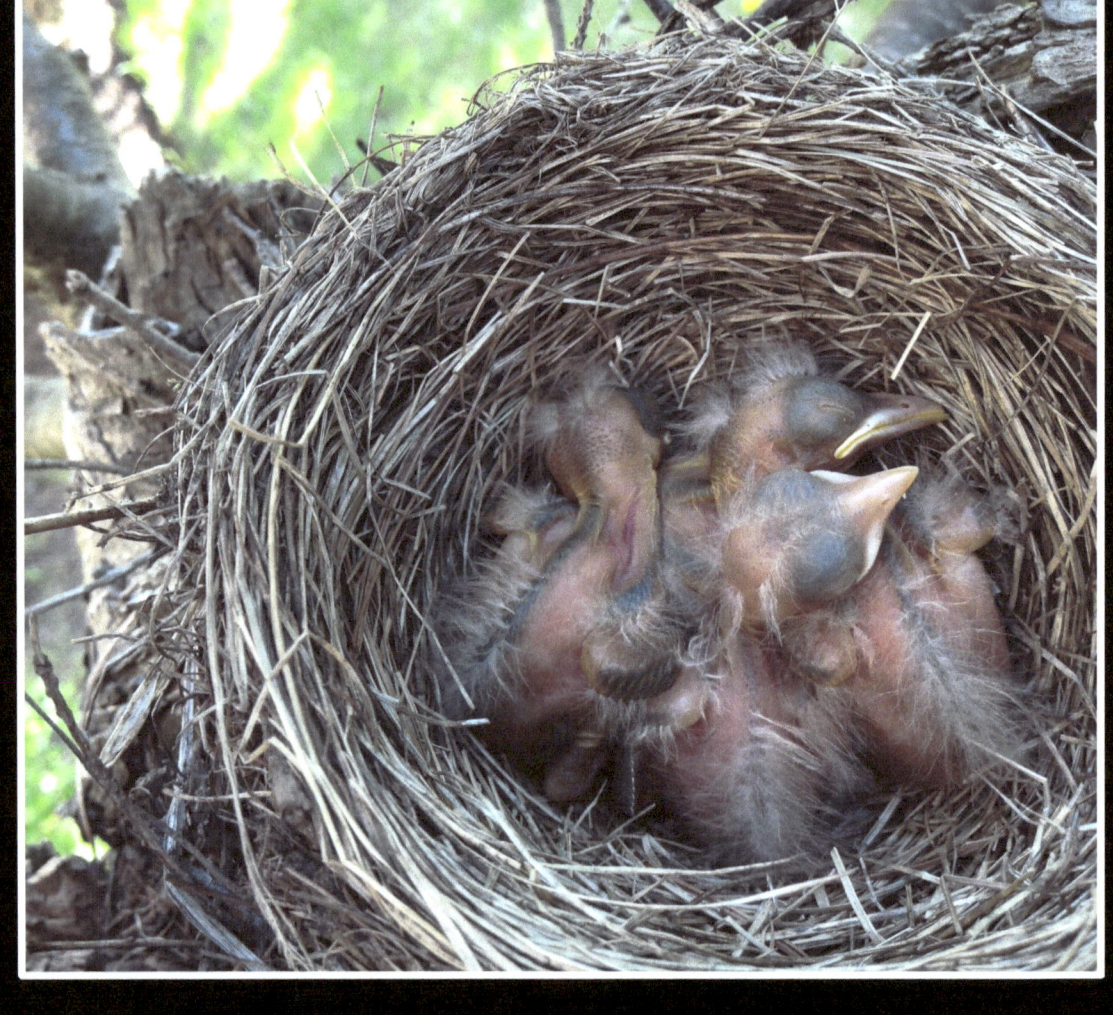

When I first looked at the chicks on the start of day four, they were so twisted together that I wondered if only three had survived. When I counted their spines I realized one was hiding its head.

For the first four days of their lives, robin nestlings eat only food that their parents regurgitate for them. Tomorrow they will start to get broken bits of worms and insects.

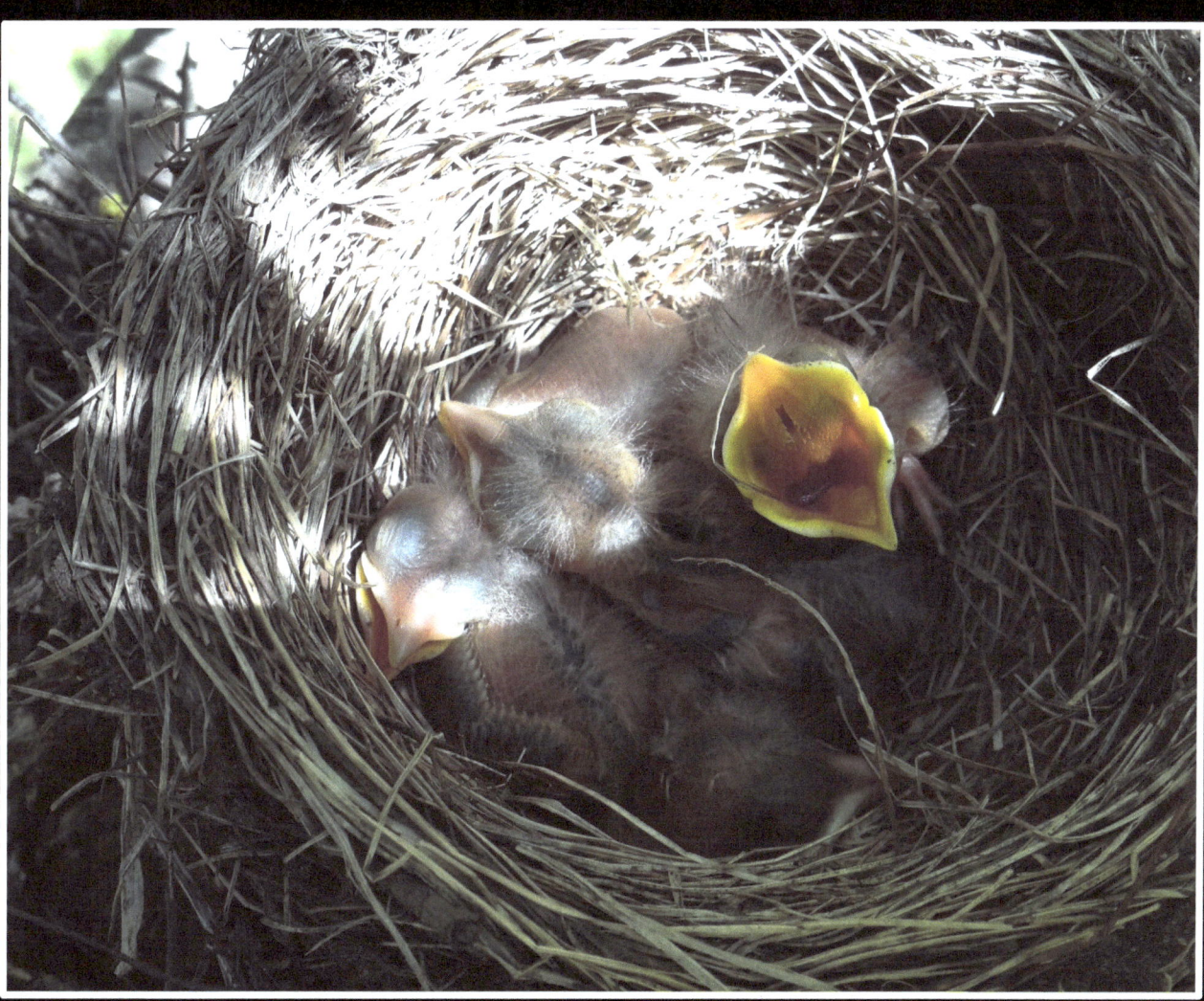

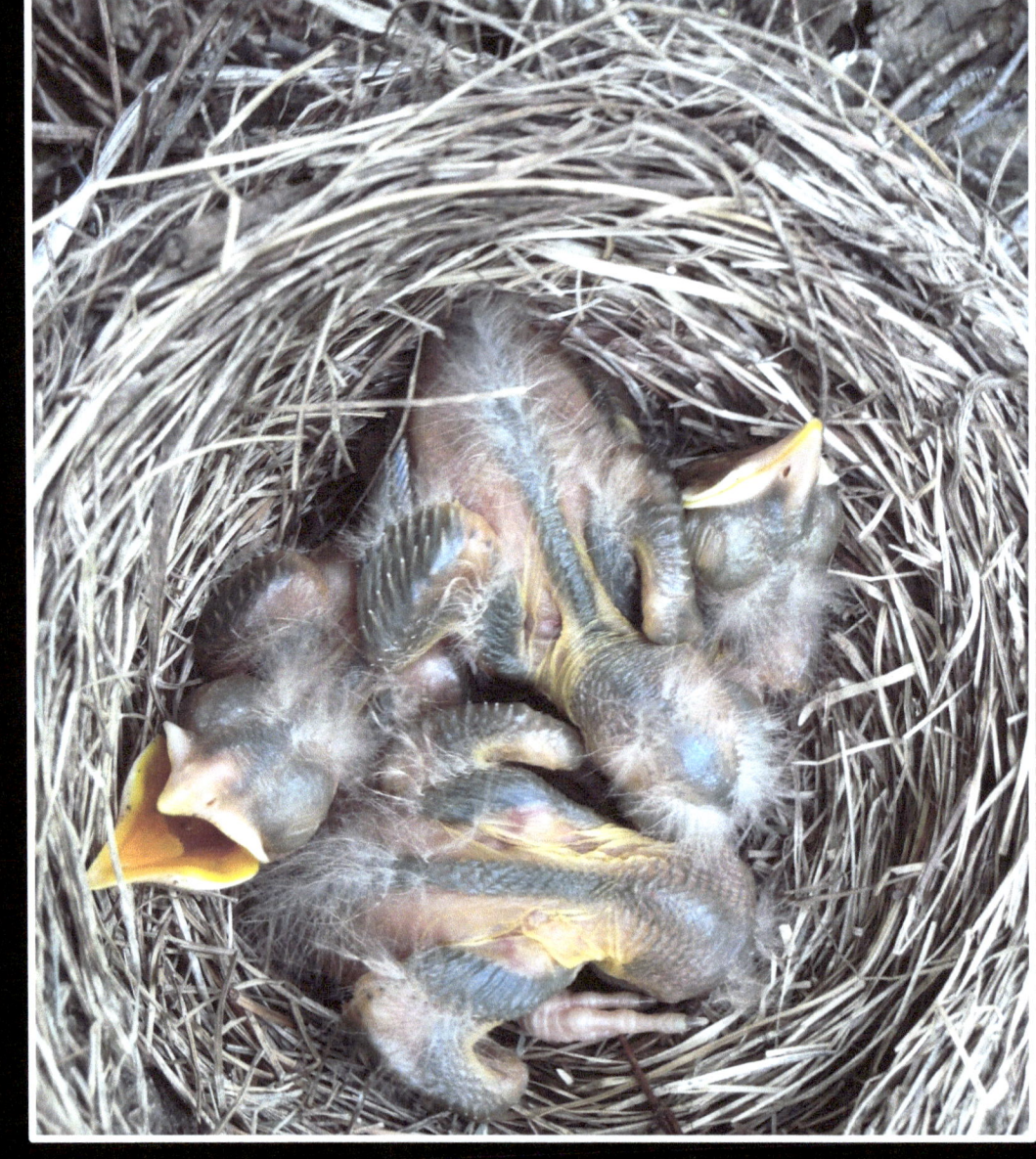

Look at the little wings!

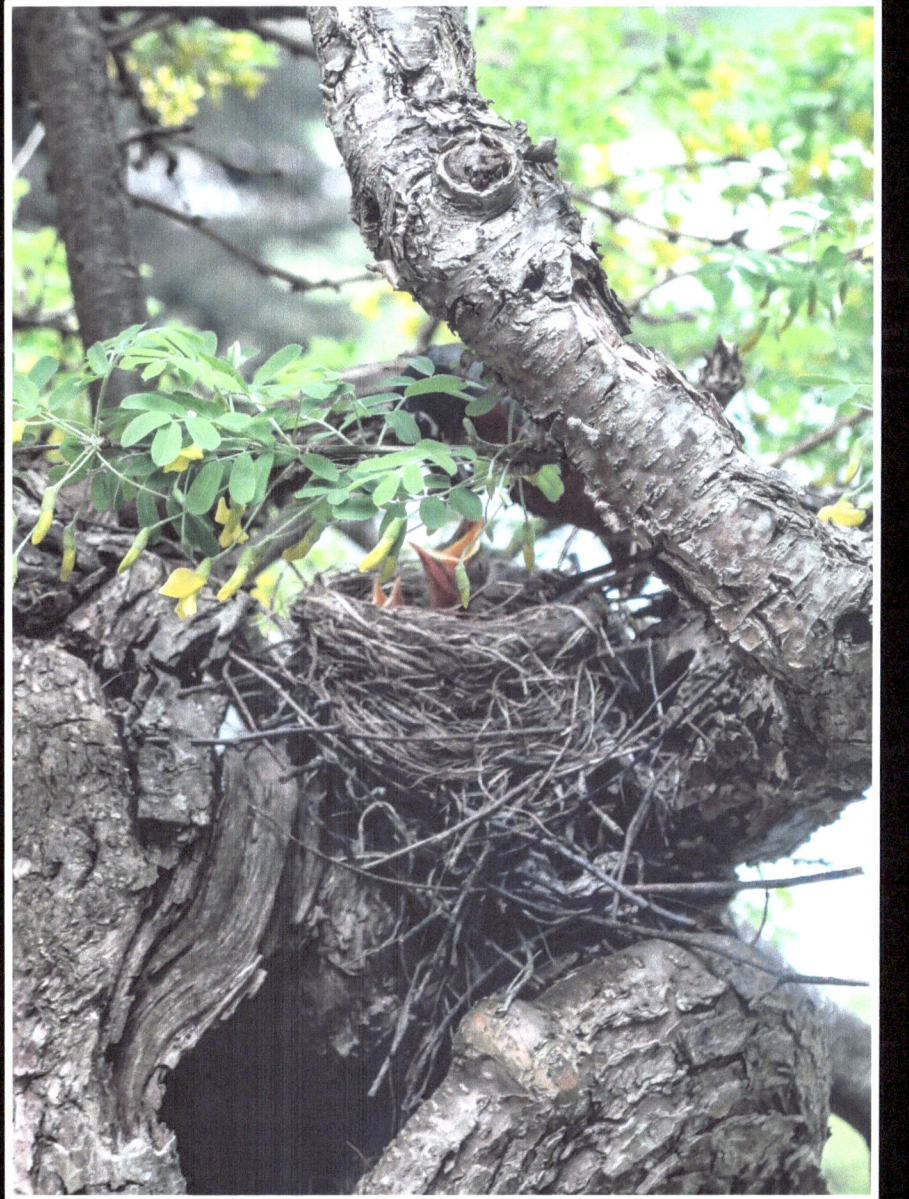

And the little eyes!

Baby robins sit very still unless they feel the bounce of their parents landing on the nest, or see the shadow their parents cast when they land over them. Then they beg for food!

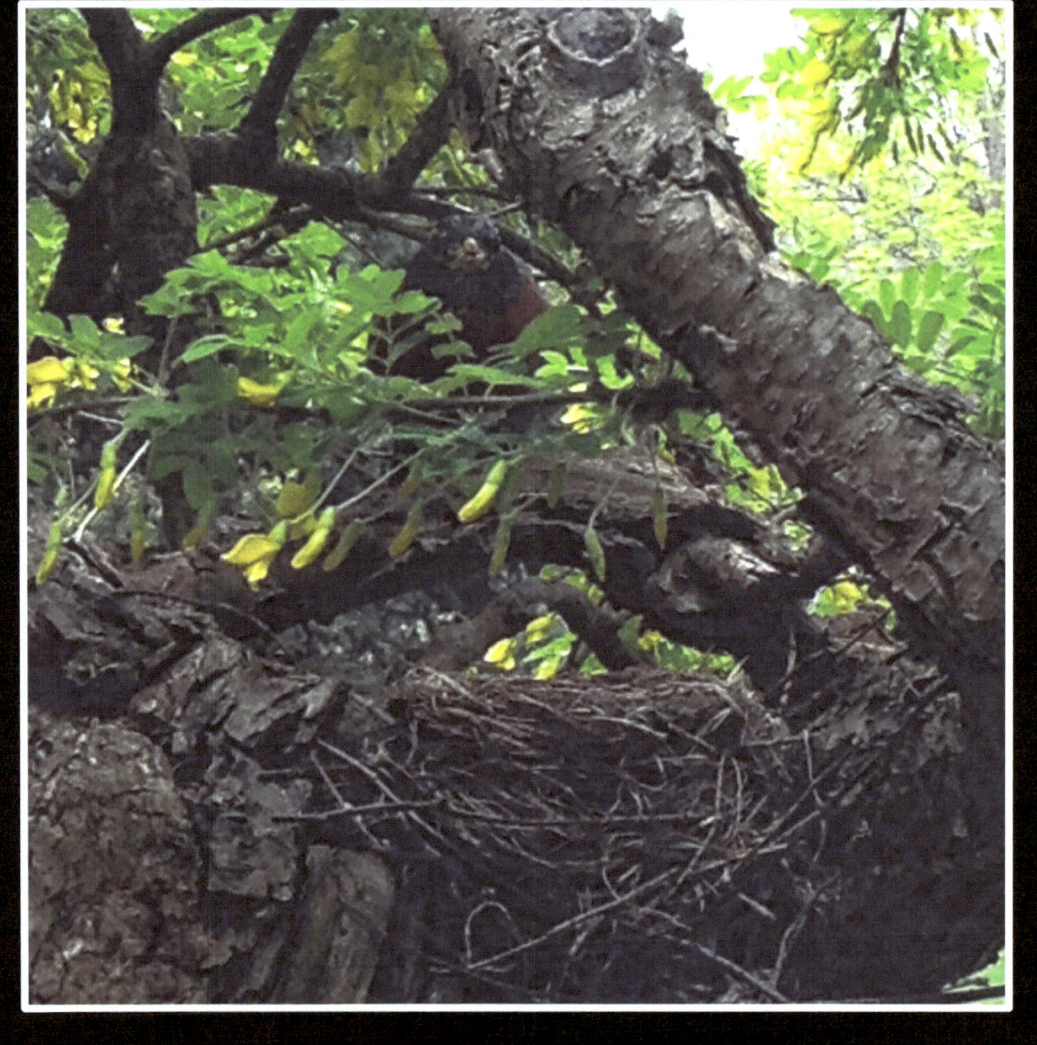

Robins have short flight-initiation-distance. That means nothing can get very close before they fly away. Sometimes, though, they'll puff themselves up to try to look scary to try to frighten away a dangerous predator

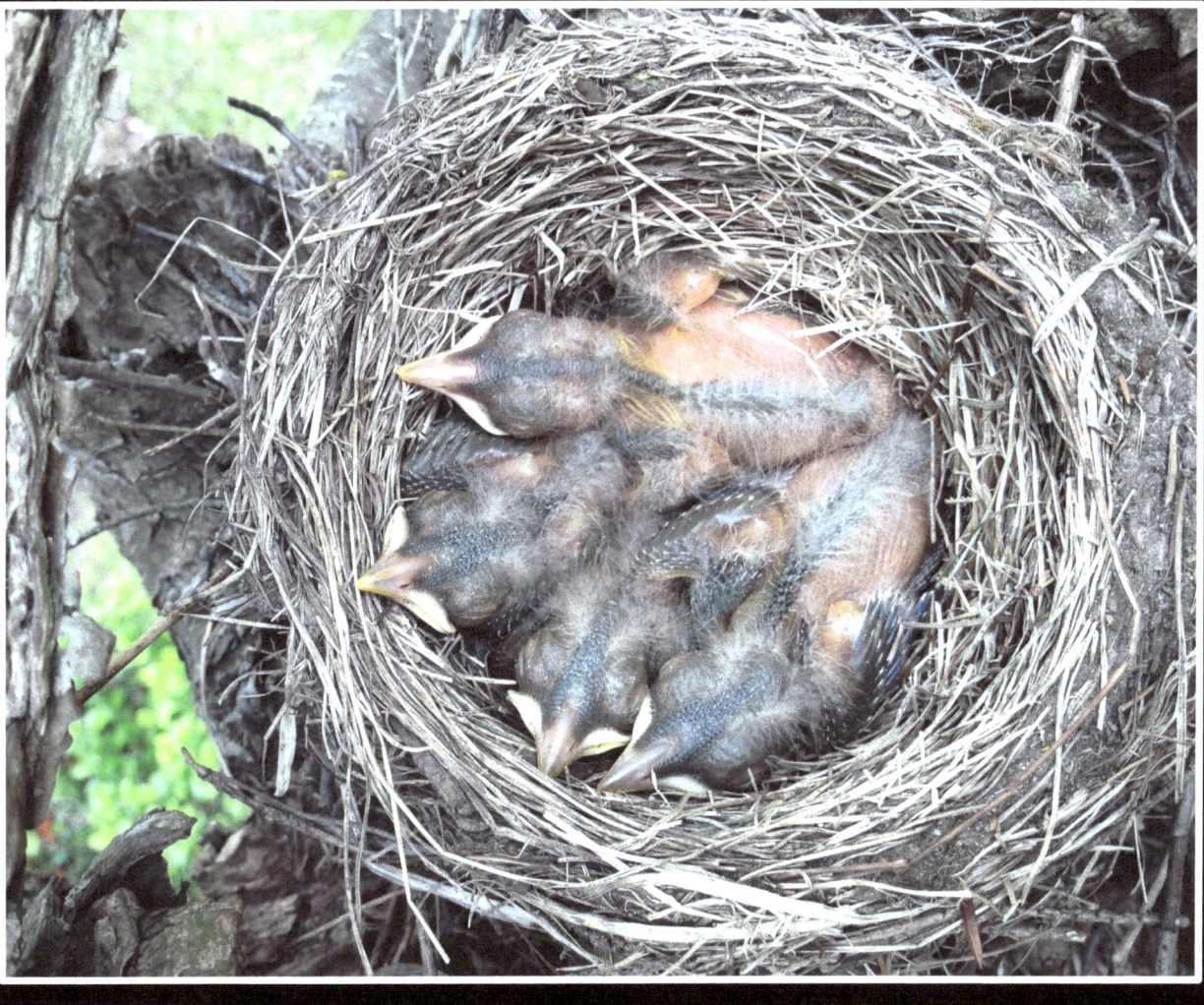

It was amazing to see the tiny feathers growing out of the nestlings' wings!

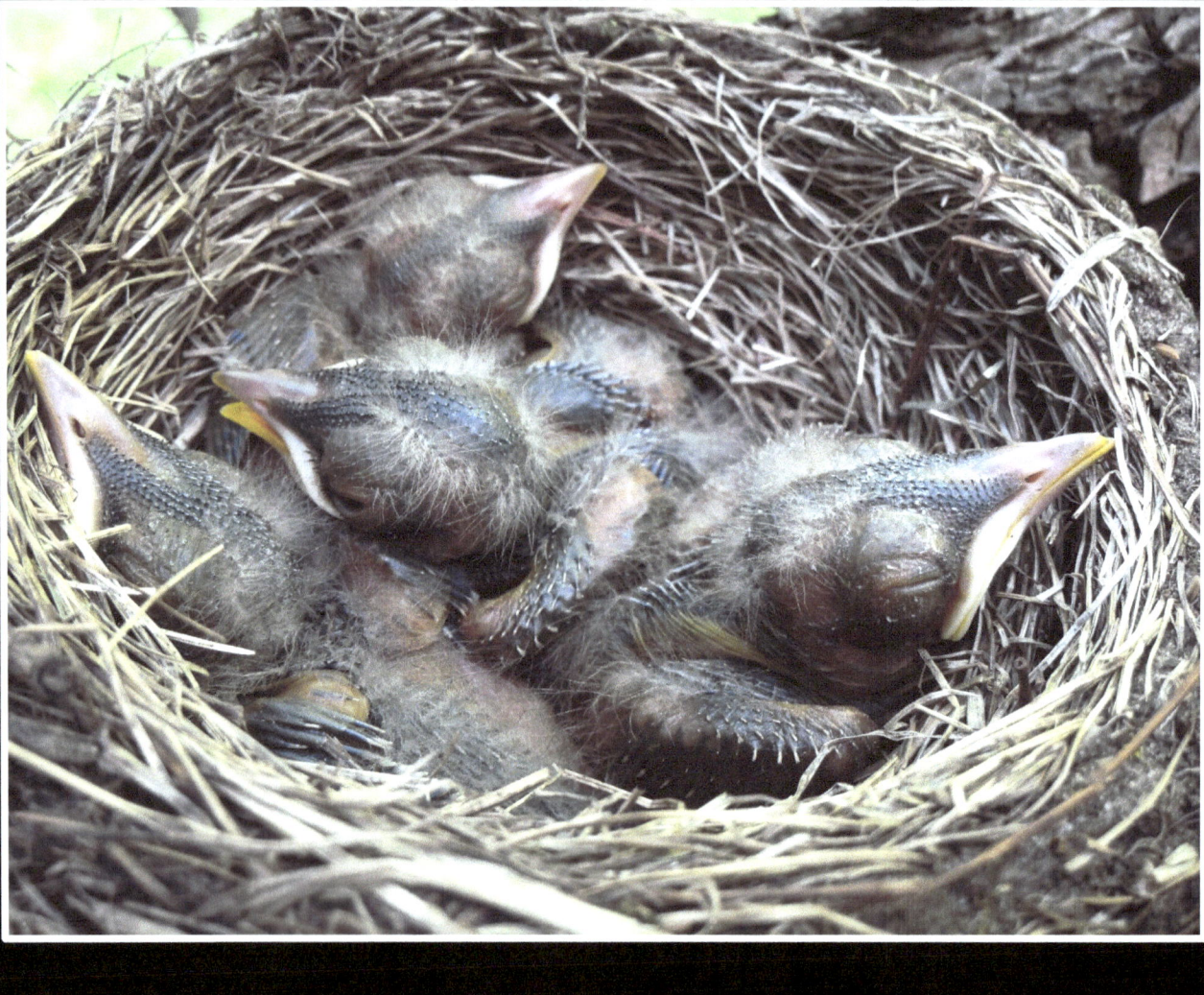

The chicks need this long for their eyes to begin to open. Their ear-holes had been open for longer - they are just below and behind their eyes. Soon the chicks will grow feathers over these holes to protect their ears from the wind.

Robin bird parents have to feed their babies as often as every 10 to 20 minutes during the day! Even when they were off the nest these two were never very far away!

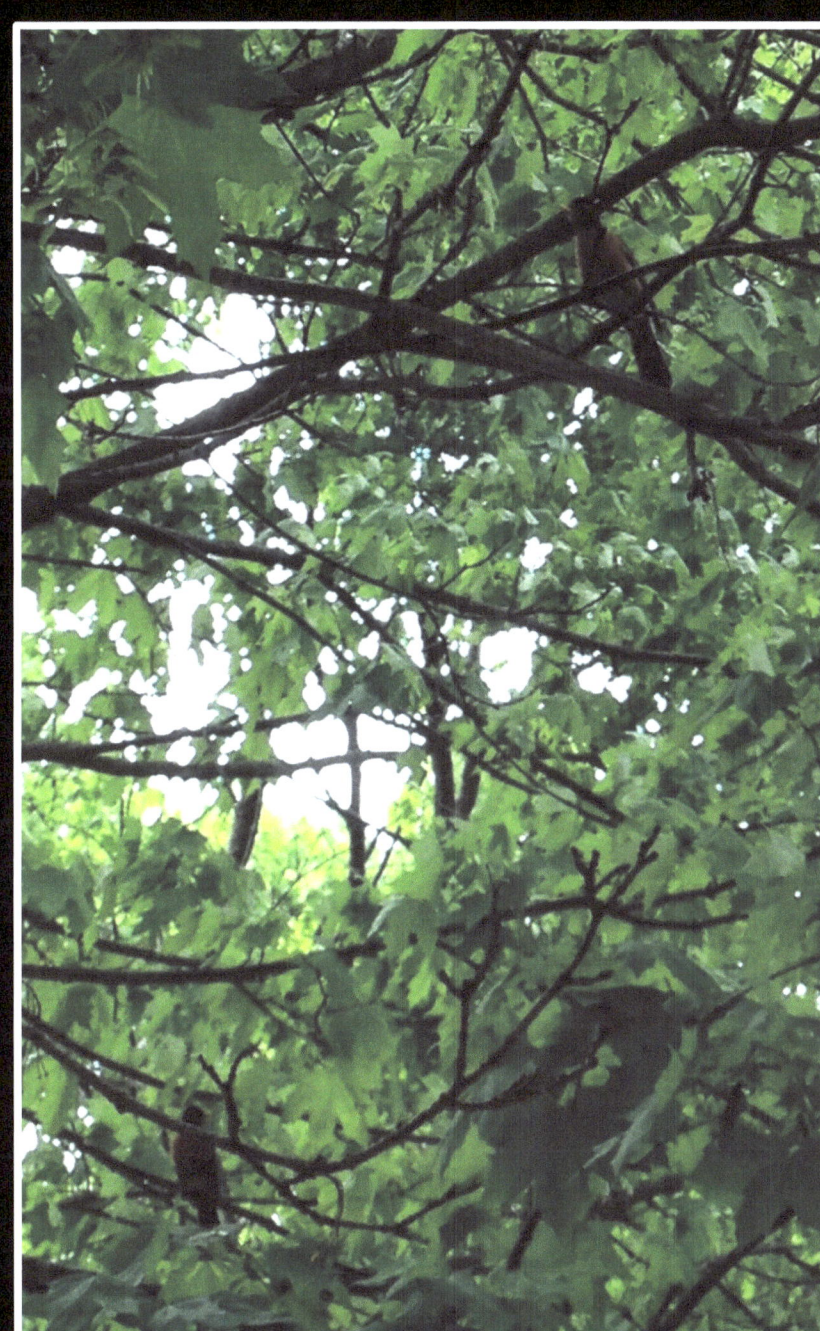

On the morning of their seventh day, the chicks looked like birds—their eyes were open and they had far more feathers.

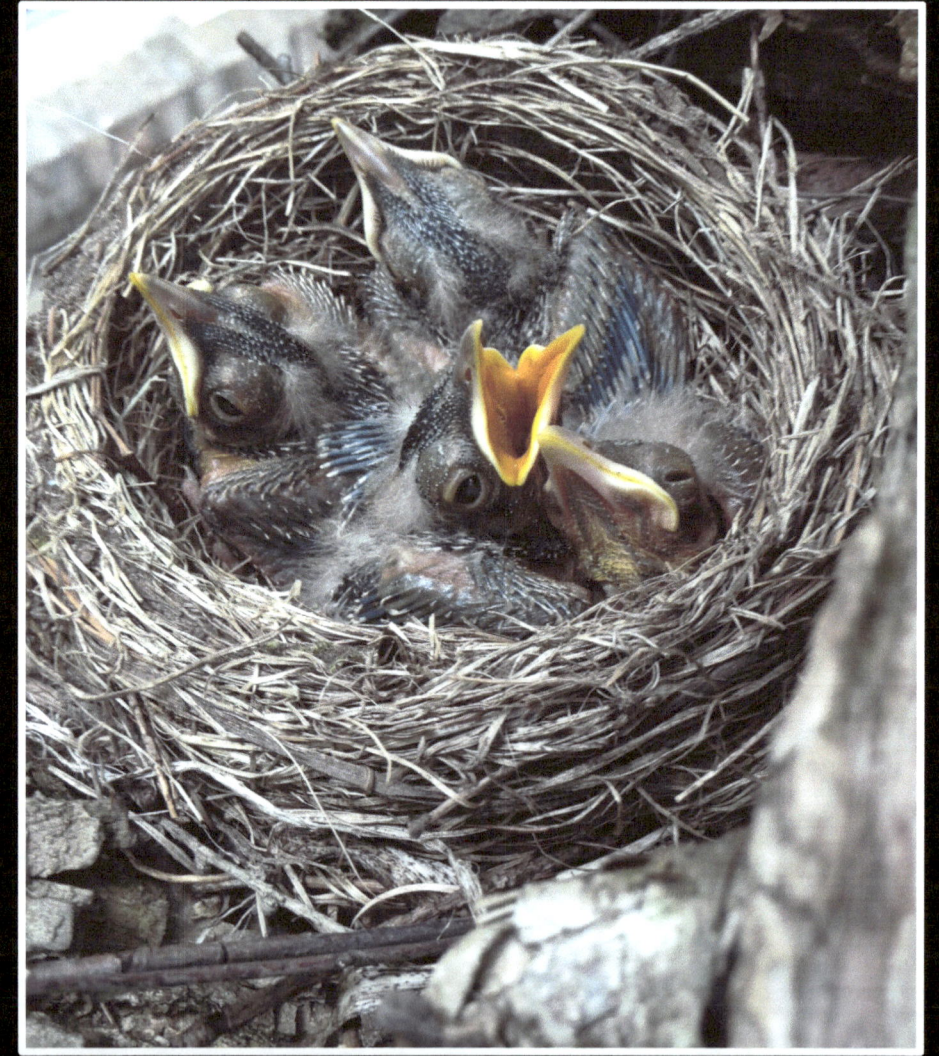

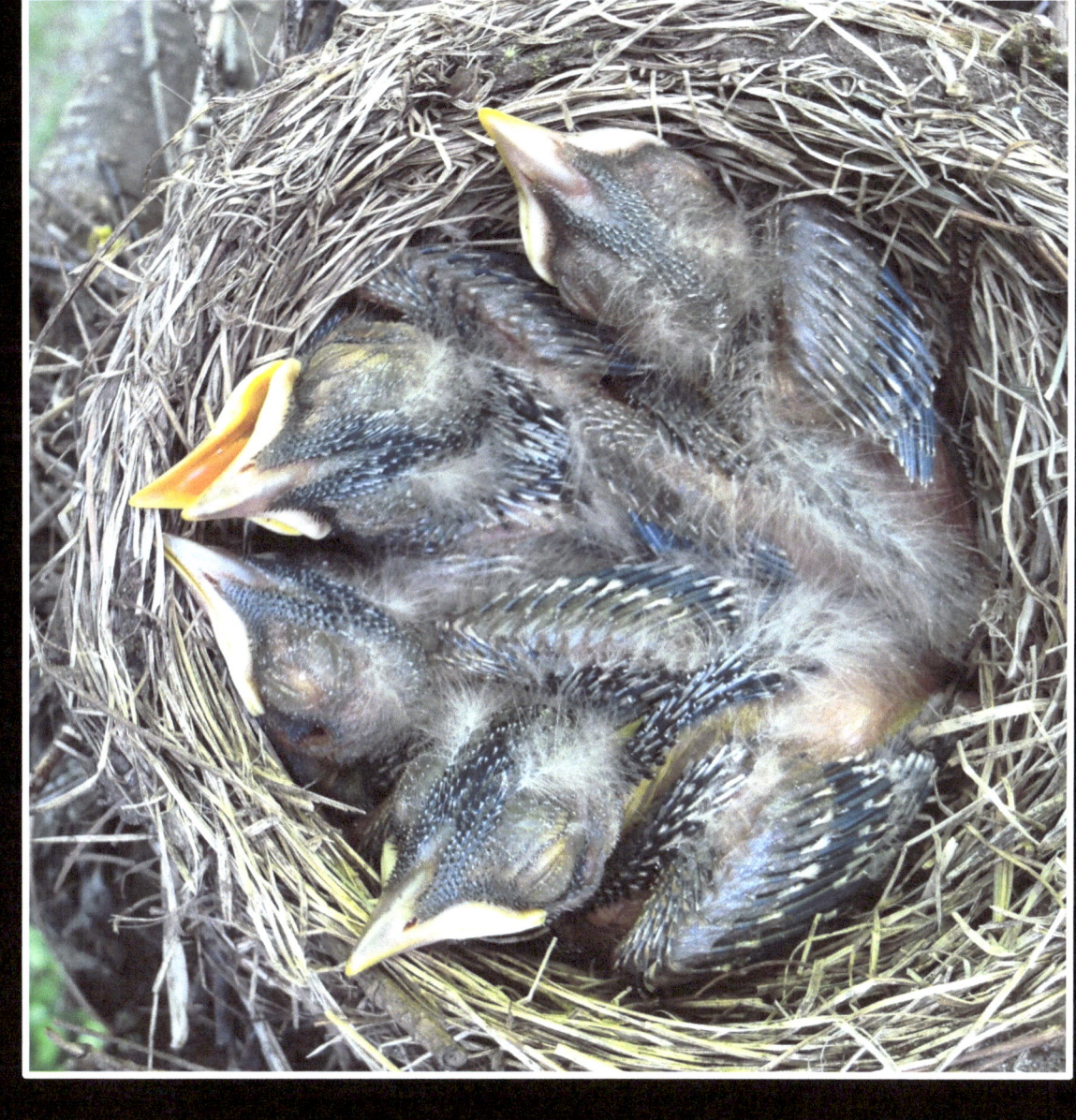

When feathers come in, they look like little straws unti
the protective sheath breaks off and the feathers fluff
out.

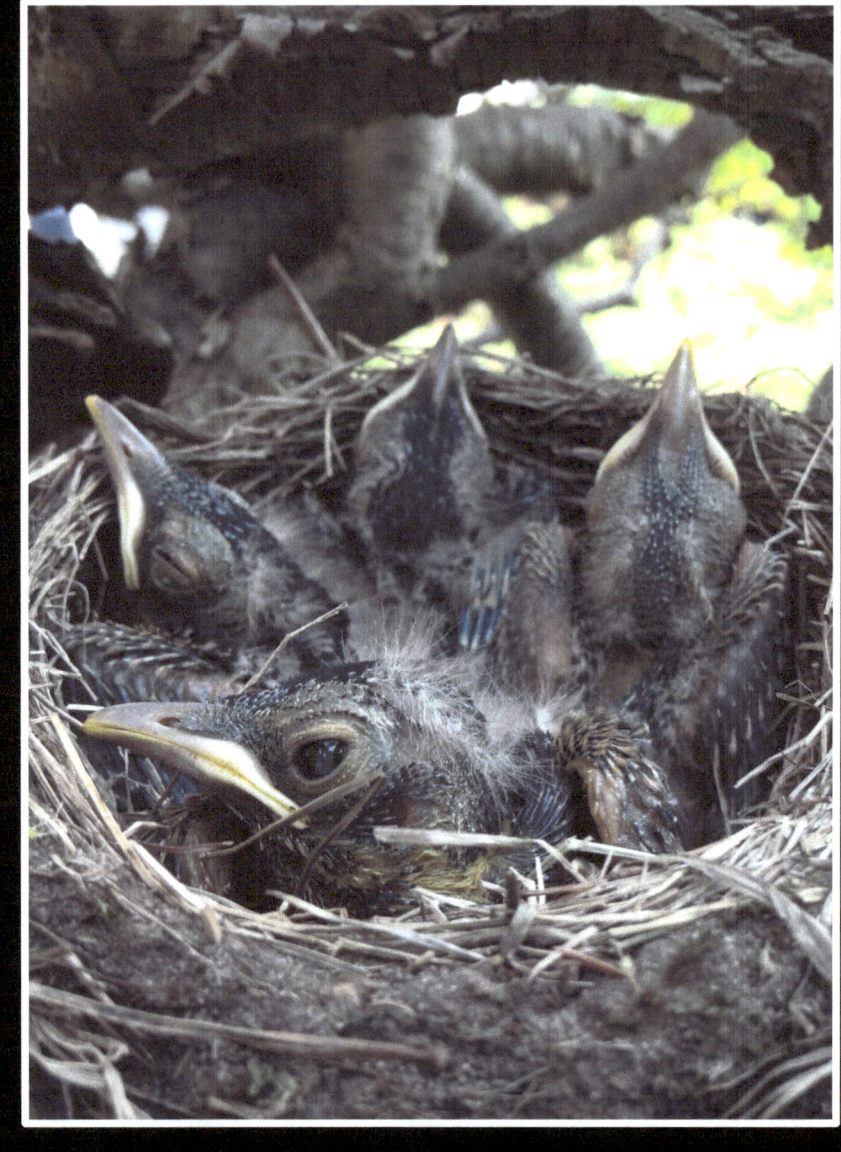

One week old!

Growing babies need food. Lots and lots of food!

Even though the chicks poop immediately after each feeding, all of their poop is encased in a membrane to keep the nest from getting too messy. The robin parents pick up the poop and carry it away from the nest.

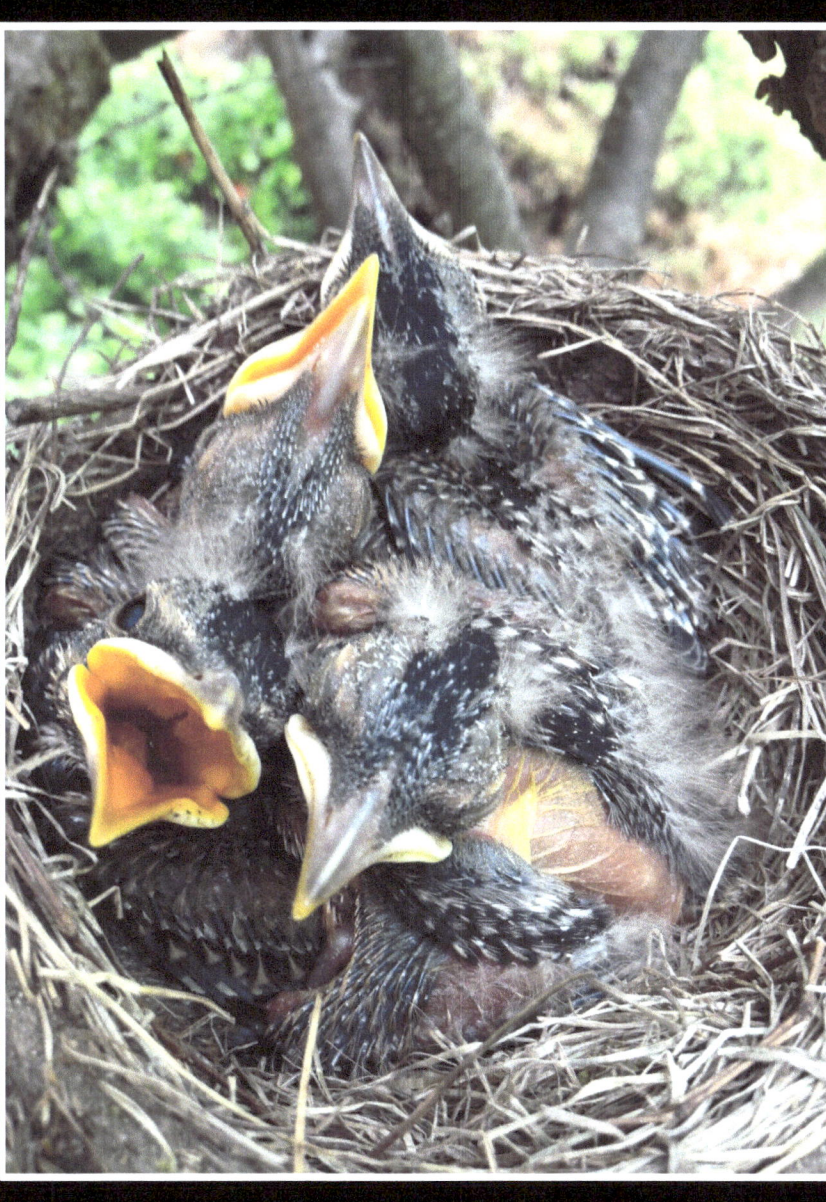

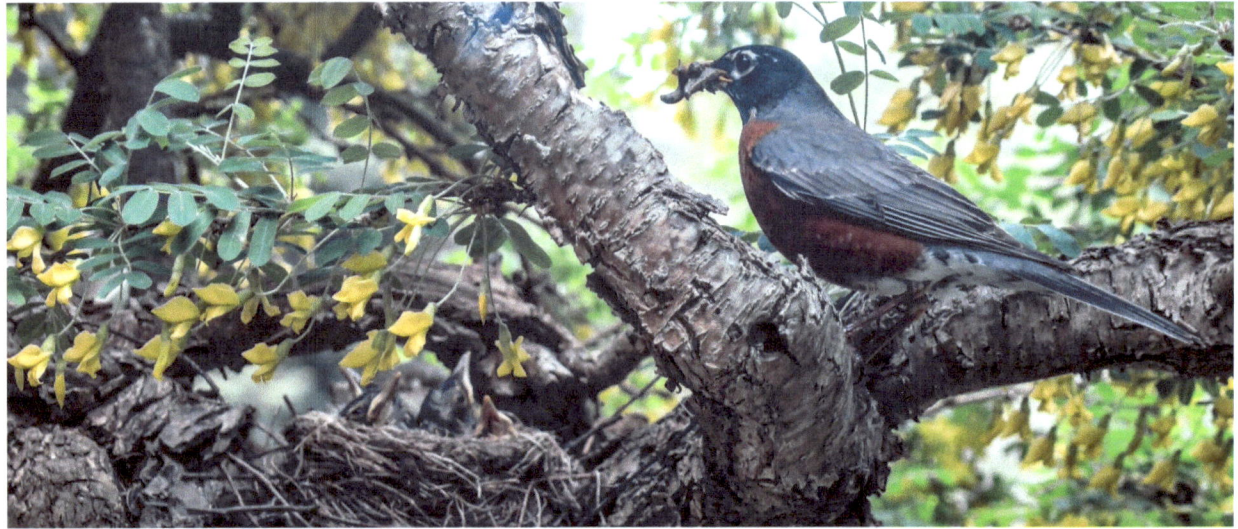

This kind of robin is also called the American robin, or the Red-Breasted robin, and it only lives in North America. In Europe there is another kind of robin which is much smaller.

It was easy to see that these little creatures are the closest living relative to dinosaurs!

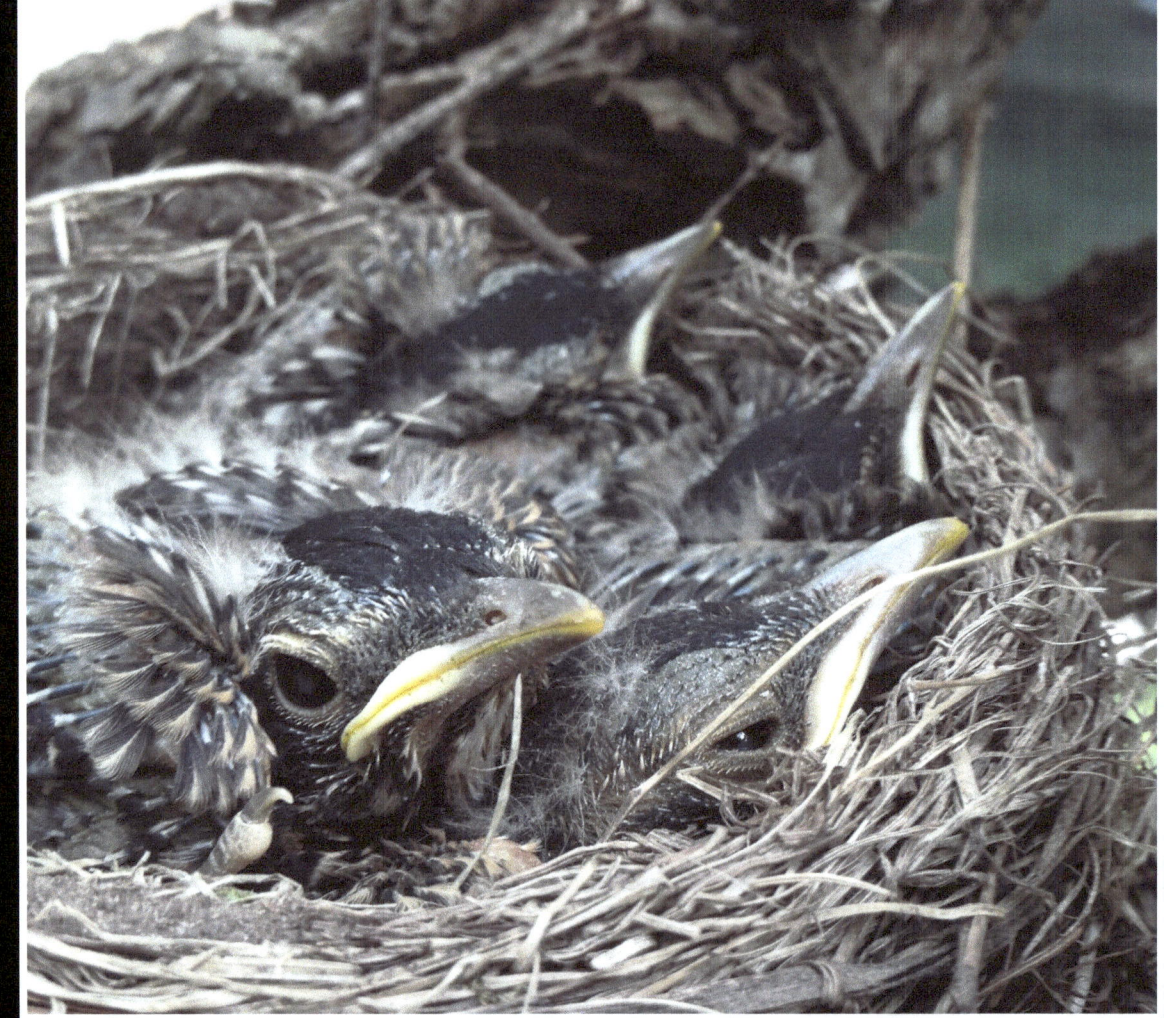

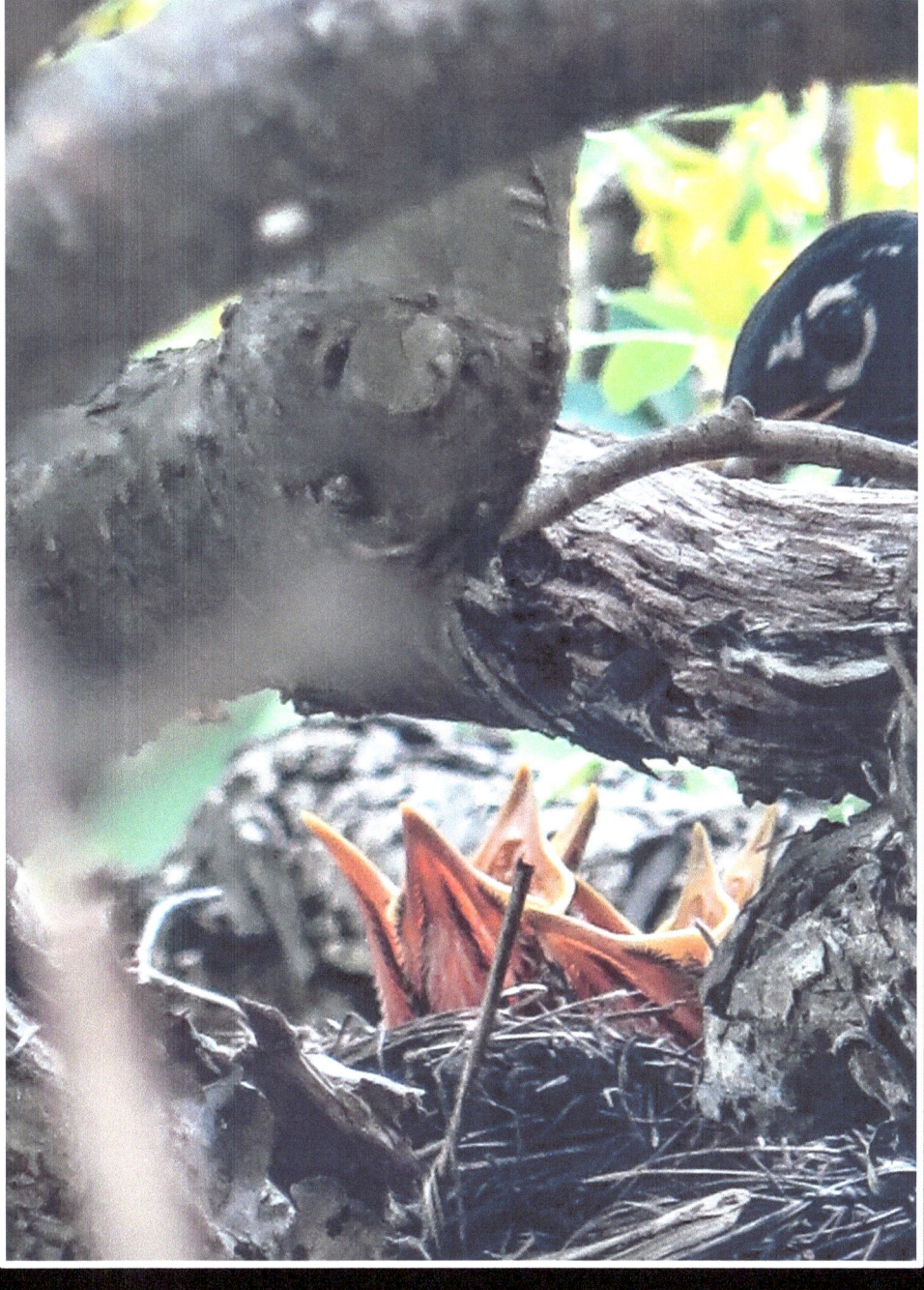

When the air was chilly, the chicks snuggled up together and faced the sunshine for added warmth

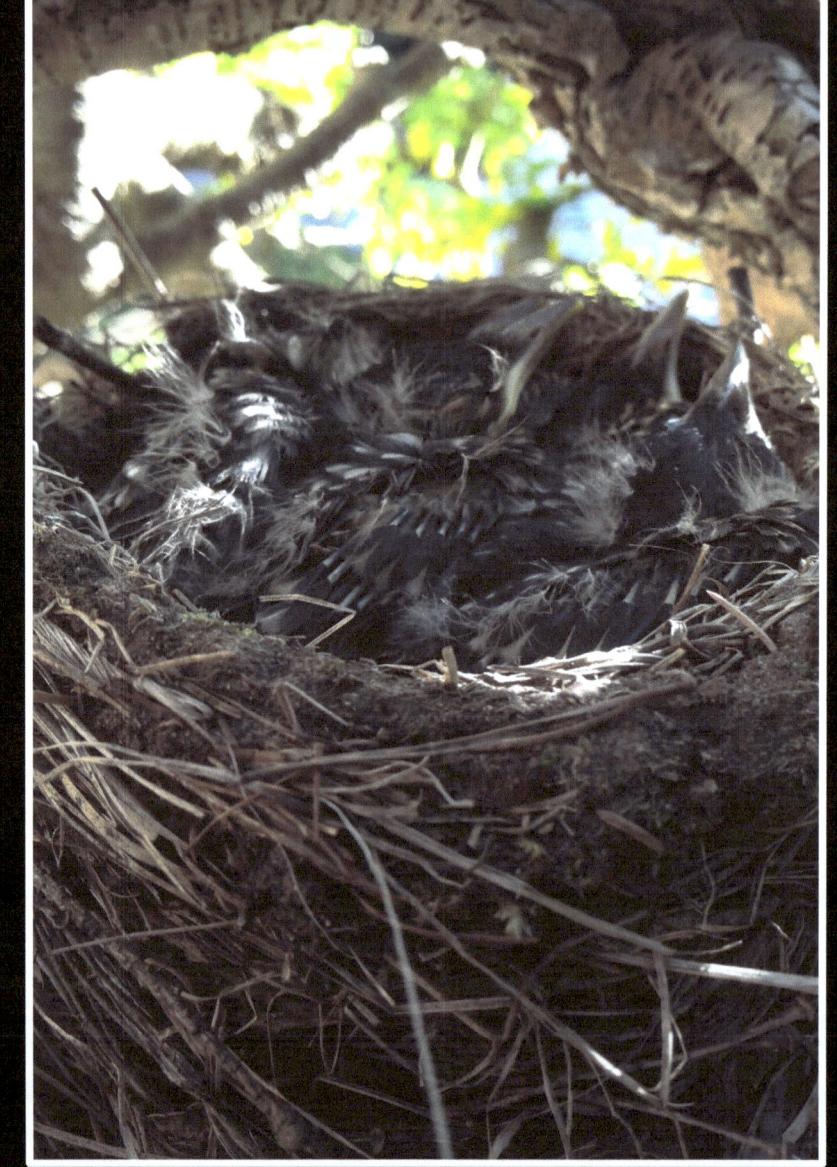

The chicks' soft, downy feathers kept them warm, too.

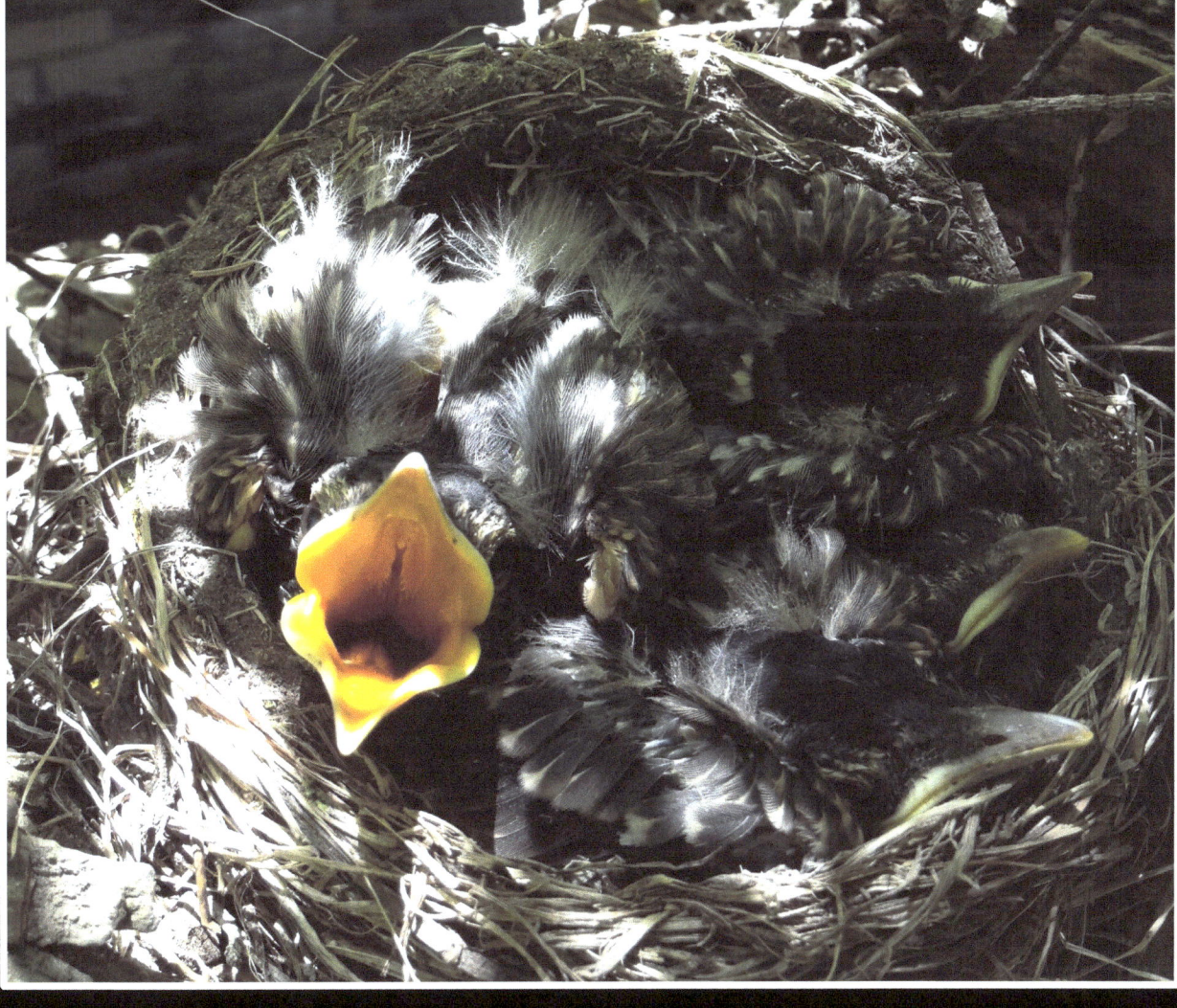

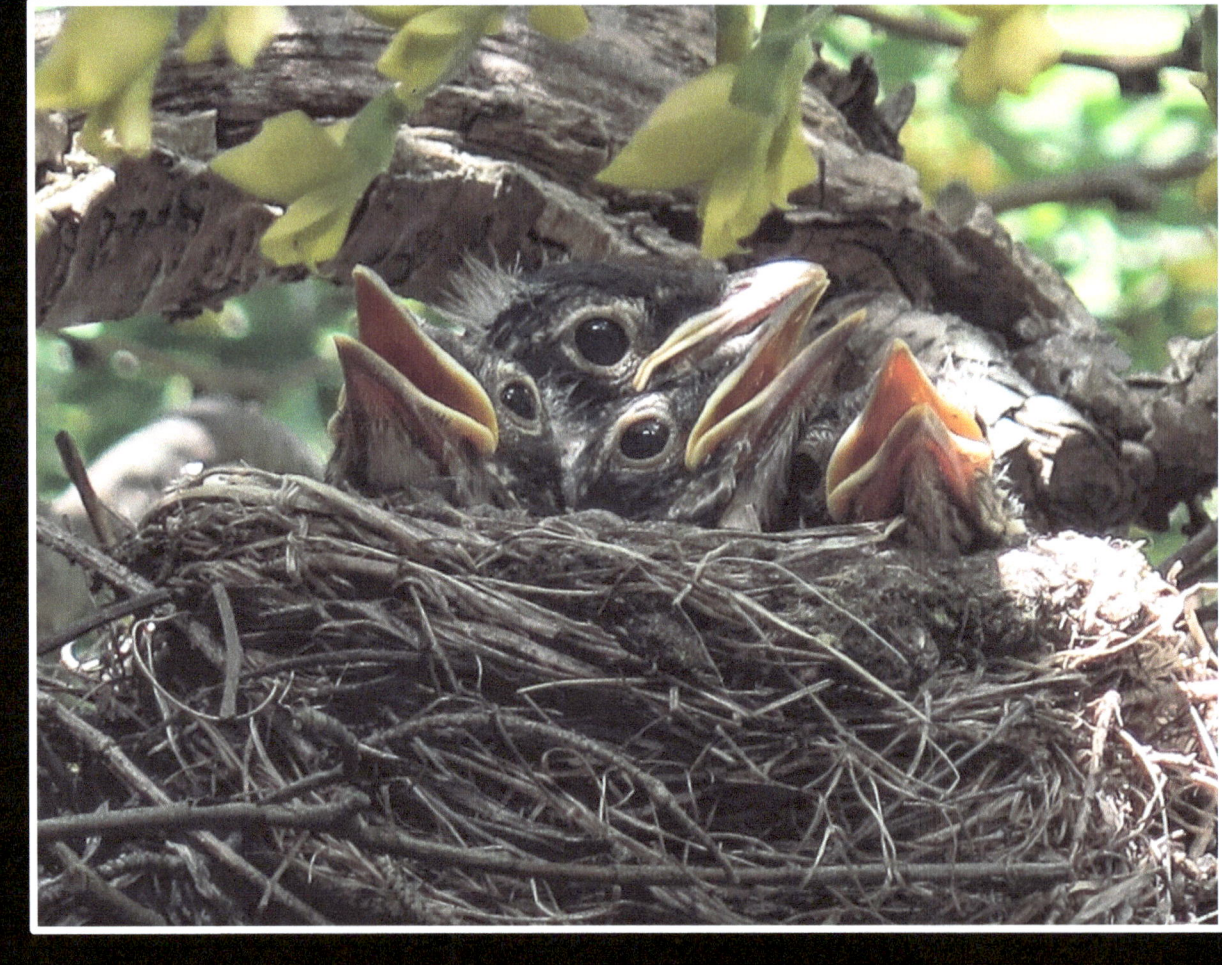

When the chicks were born, they weighed about 5.5 grams - that's lighter than a quarter. By now, they were fast approaching their parents' weight of about 77 grams. That's a lot of growing in 11 days!

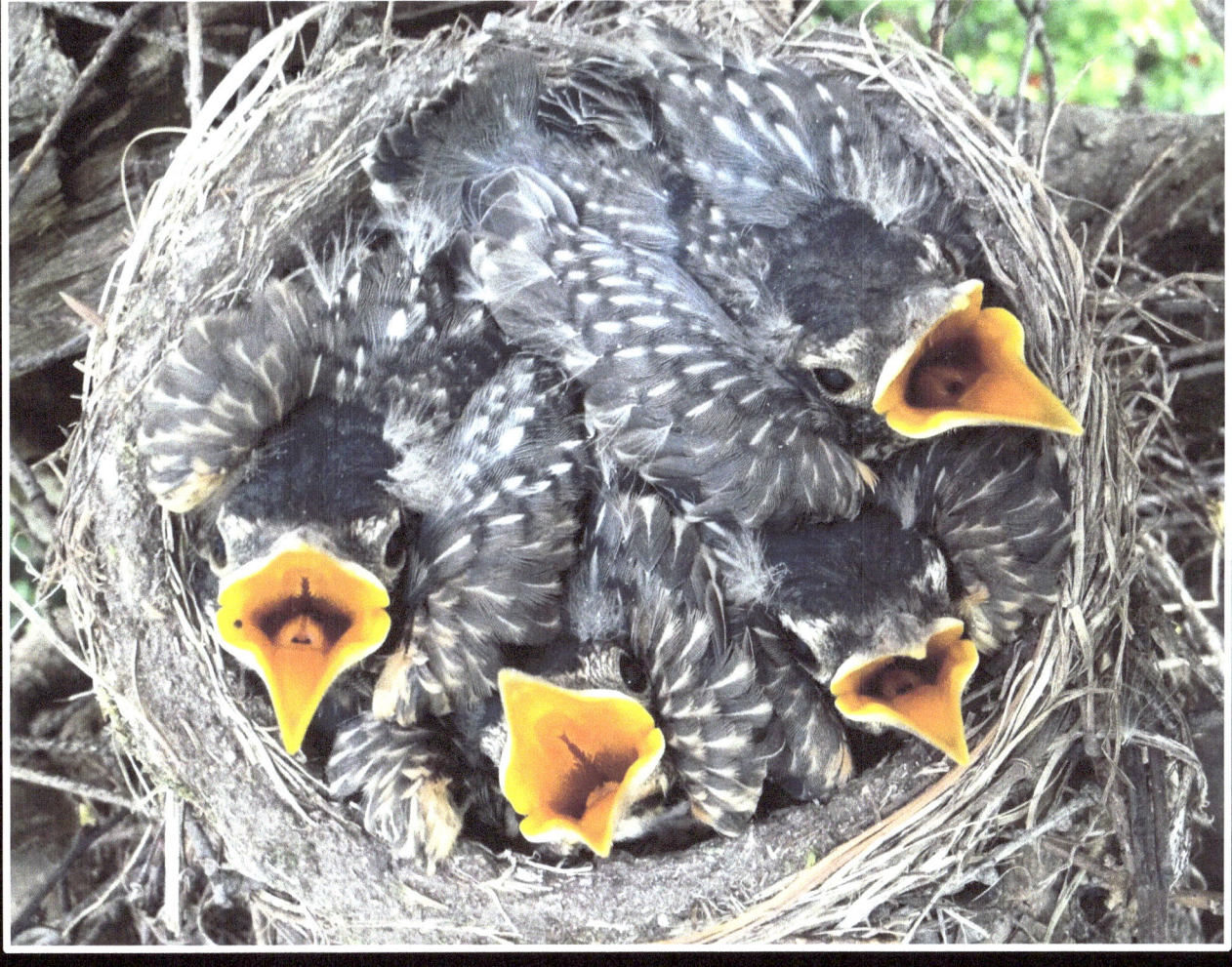

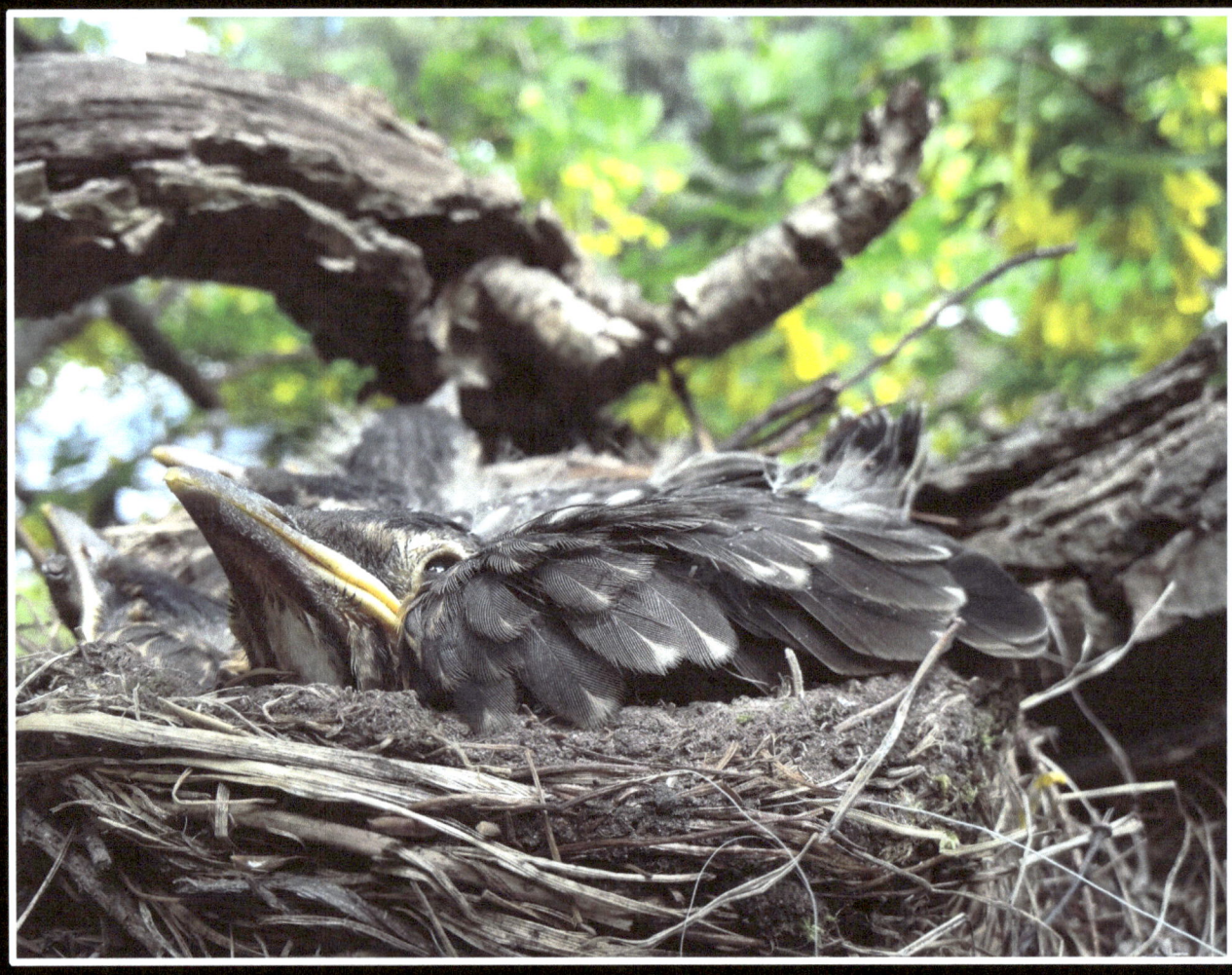

The chicks' flight feathers were nearly ready. Flight feathers are the long feathers with uneven edges on the wings and tail, and all birds need them to fly.

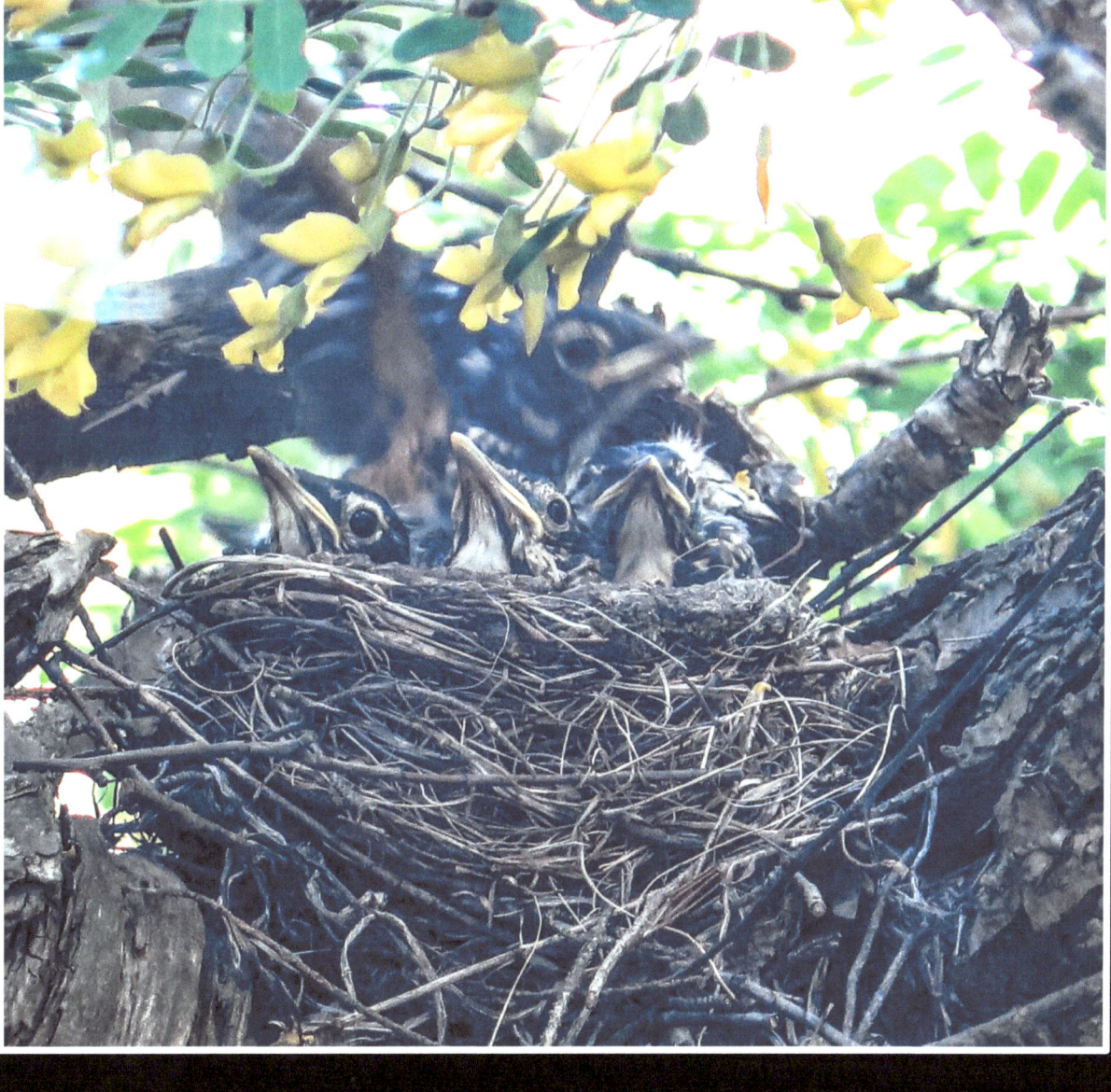

When the chicks start stretching their wings they are no longer called nestlings but fledglings.

By now the chicks were so big that their mother no longer needed to sleep with them to keep them warm.

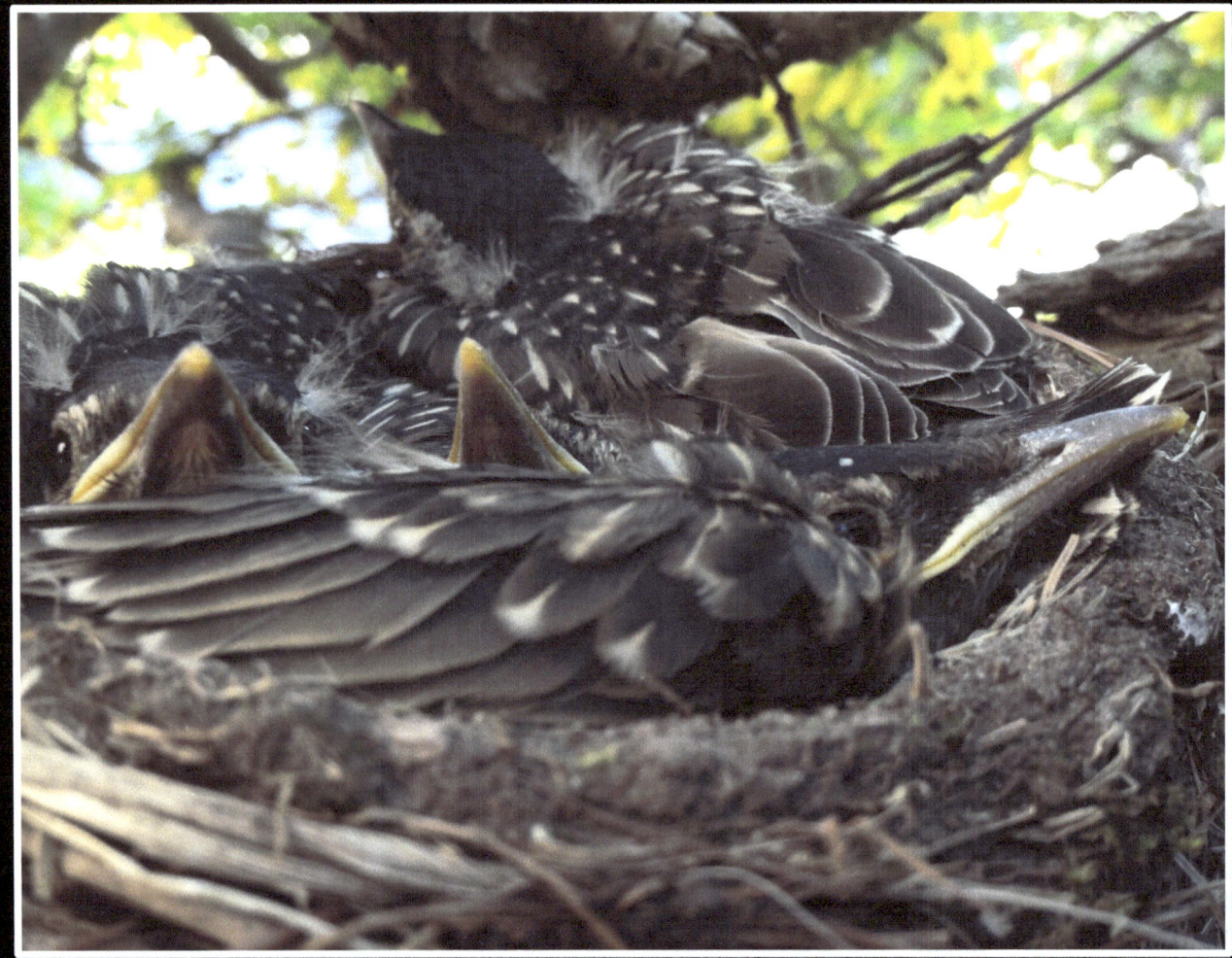

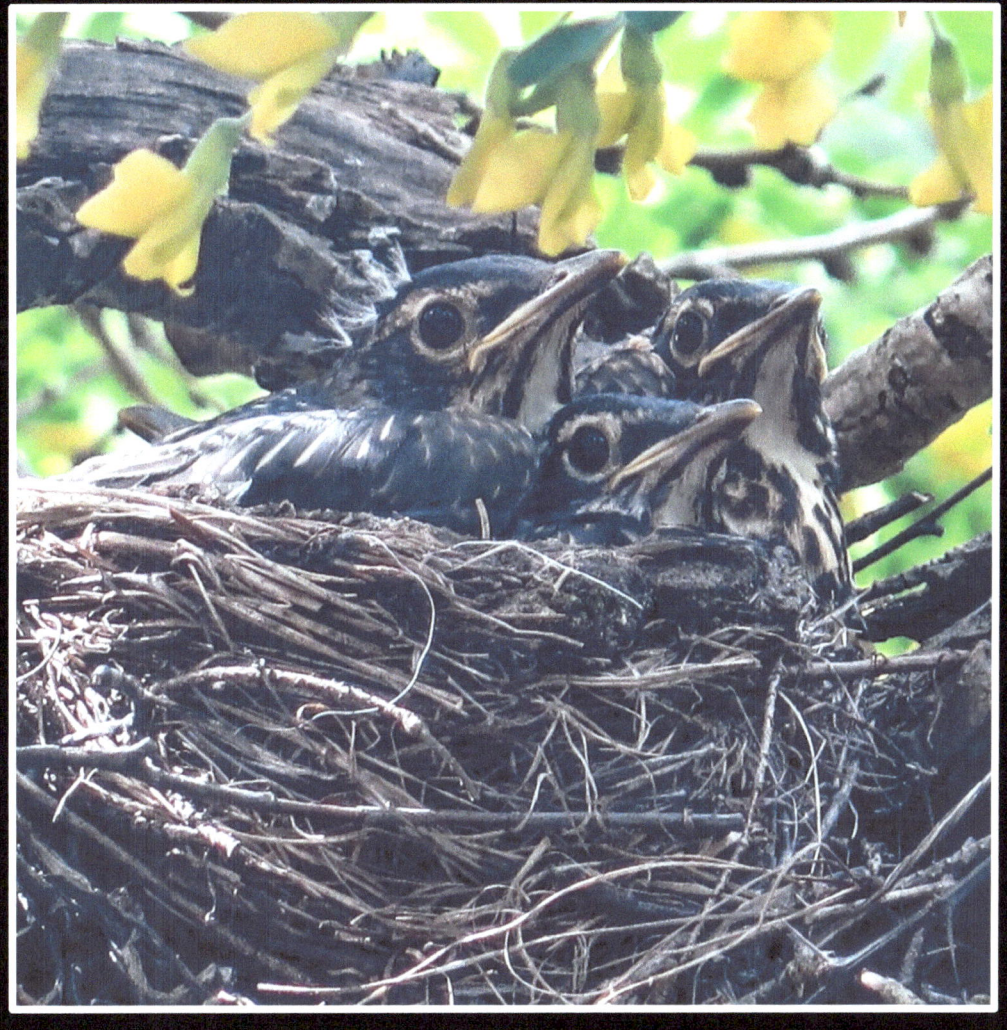

The fledglings were now perching up high in the nest, trying to work up the nerve to jump out.

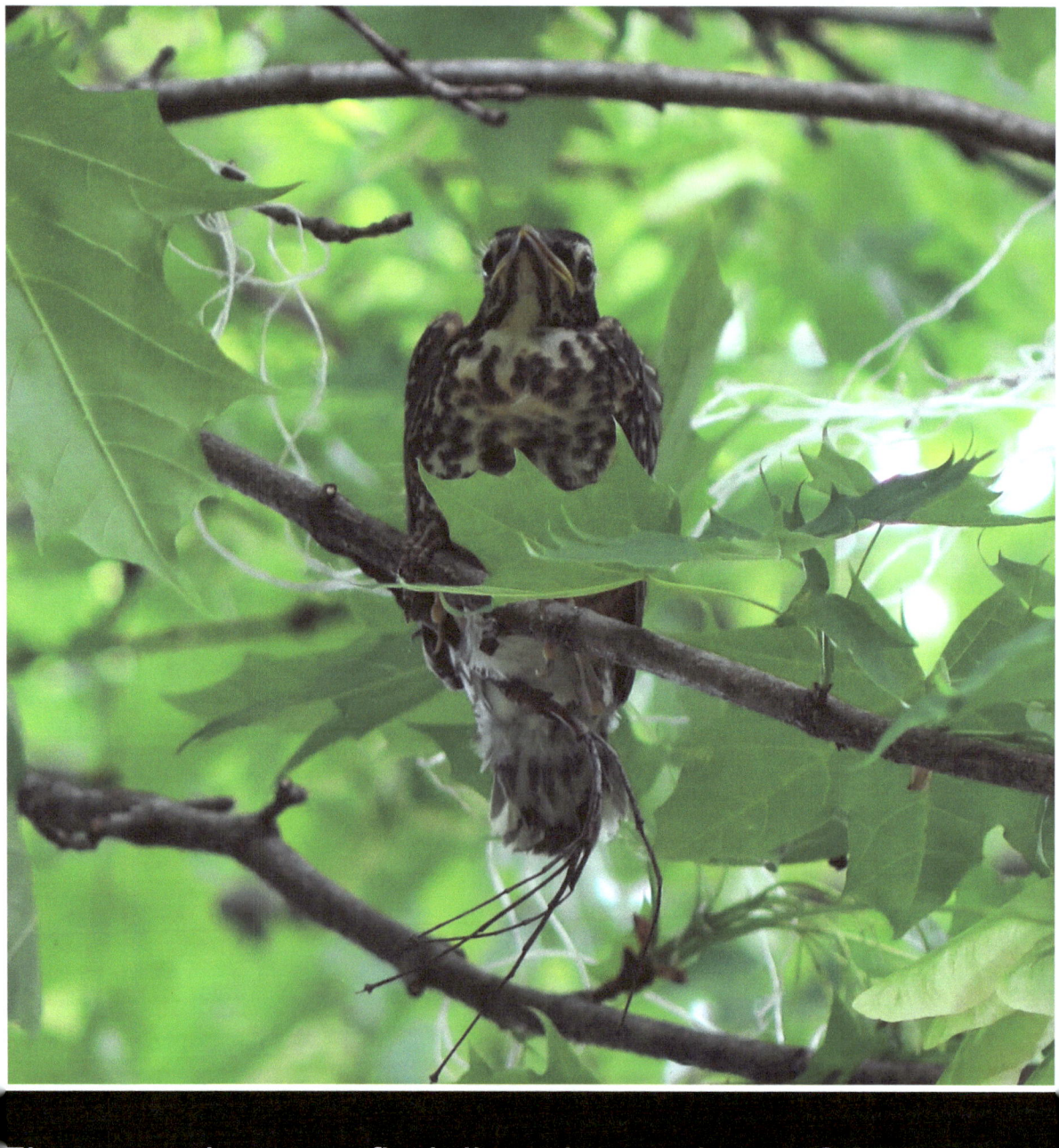

First one, then two fledglings jumped out of the nest and flew for the first time! This one is likely a female as they tend to have less red on their chests

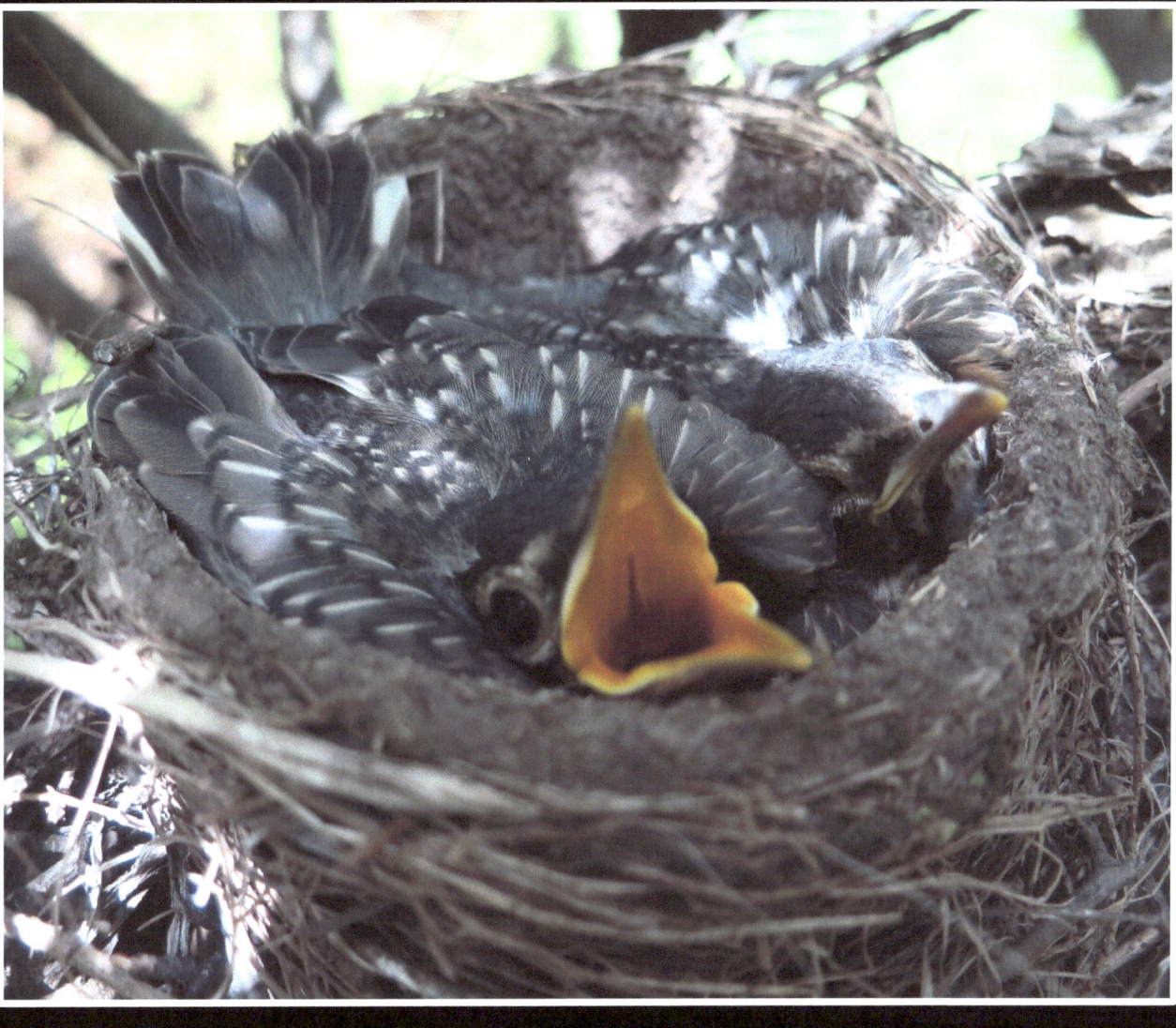

The last two needed a little more time still. These were likely the two that hatched last so they needed a few extra hours to get ready.

DAY 15

When I first looked out the window in the morning of day 15, there were still two chicks in the nest. Just a few minutes later, the nest was empty and I found the last fledgling hiding in the leaves of a nearby tree.

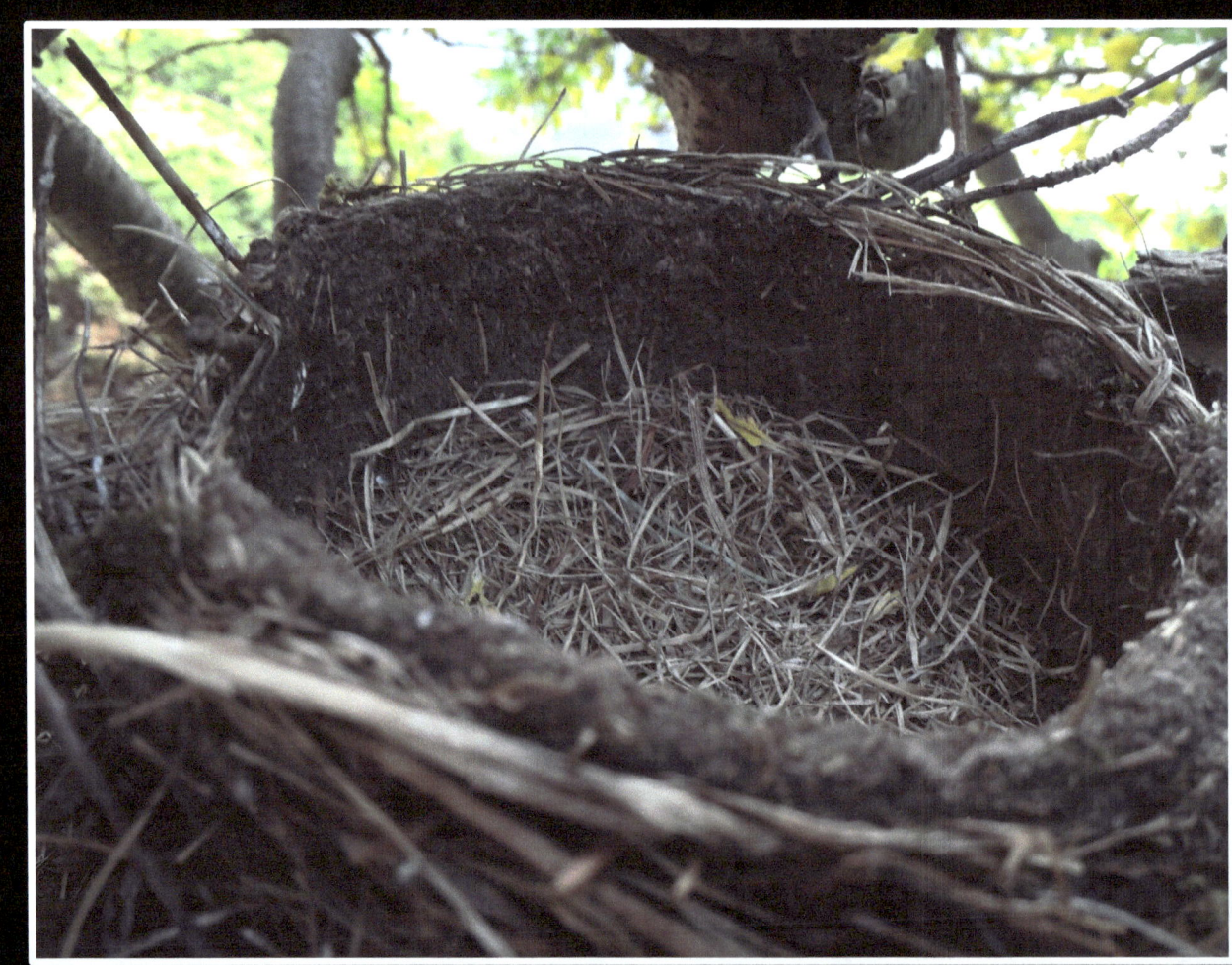

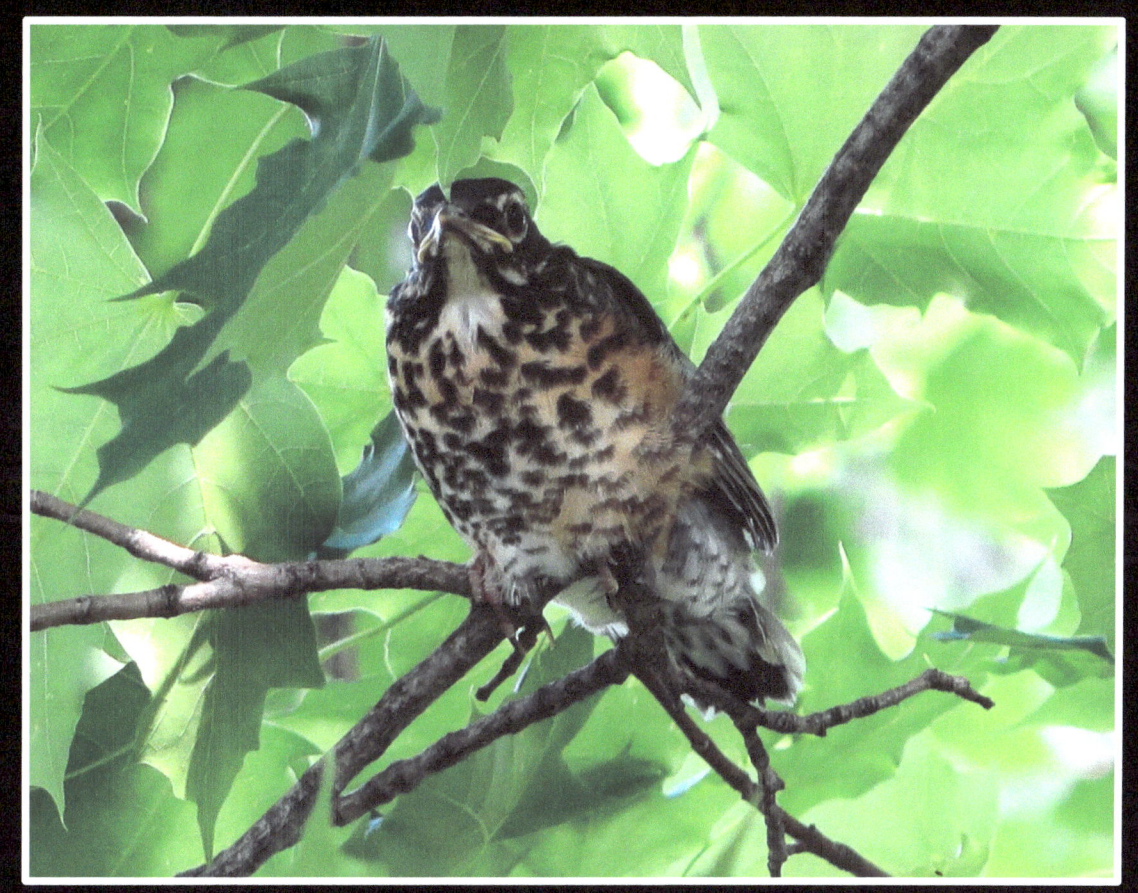

All four of these little chicks will follow both their parents for the next two weeks while they learn to hunt and protect themselves. After that, their mother will likely lay two more clutches of eggs. Their father will keep watching over the young birds until the new chicks hatch. These little birds will continue to learn from other robins for the next year and then they will be able to have babies of their own.

About these photos:

Birds get very nervous if their eggs are disturbed and can sometimes abandon their nest if they think they are at risk. It was important for me not to stay at the nest too long or too often.

I took these pictures in two ways: For the close up shots, I reached my hands up over my head and took pictures on my iPhone without actually seeing what I was focusing on. I am not a professional photographer so did not set up a tripod or use a zoom lens. I just kept visiting and trying not to irritate the parents by staying too long. Every time I went to the nest, one of the parents would chirp loudly at me from a nearby tree so i knew they were protecting their babies. The pictures of the parents and the trees I took with my Canon G16 camera, sometimes from inside my living room, sometimes from outside in the yard.

Taking all of these photos and following the birds was a lovely surprise gift for our family when we discovered the nest of the Mother's Day weekend 2015! Photos taken May 11 - May 25, 2015.

www.ingramcontent.com/pod-product-compliance
Lightning Source LLC
Chambersburg PA
CBHW051106180526
45172CB00002B/791